A Declaration
of
INDEPENDENCE

"Europe is too small for us"

Norwegian NO Campaign slogan

Published privately in 2002 in the UK by Roger Helmer

ISBN: 0 9542235 0 0

Printed in Great Britain by
Mickleprint Ltd
Westminster Road,
Vauxhall Industrial Estate,
Canterbury,
Kent CT1 1YY

Roger Helmer and Chris Heaton-Harris are Conservative
MEPs representing the East Midlands region of the UK.
They are associate members under Rule 5b of the
Parliamentary Group of the European People's Party
(Christian Democrats) and European Democrats (EPP/ED)

e-mail: rhelmer@europarl.eu.int
35 Lutterworth Road,
Blaby, Leics LE8 4DW

Phone:

UK 0116 277 9992
Brussels 00322 284 5764
Strasbourg 00333 8817 5764

Contents

Foreword

by The Rt. Hon. David Heathcoat-Amory MP

For many years most MEPs seemed to regard it as their job to represent the EU in Britain, rather than representing British interests in Europe. But in 1999 the Conservatives won the European elections and this brought in a strong group of MEPs dedicated to reversing the drift to federalism. Roger Helmer is an excellent example.

The EU is a giant political conceit, driven by an élite who are remote, expensive, arrogant and wrong. The EU is an attempt to construct a centralised European state in defiance of the principles of self-government or human-scale allegiance. Democracy at EU level is a sham: there is no European *demos* which can make a single electorate or citizenship.

Rather than float along with the tide of Euro-waffle, Roger Helmer strikes out with articles and speeches of clarity and purpose.

For instance he exposes the European gravy train where time serving officials pump out EU propaganda on inflated salaries.

He describes the myth of British 'influence' and how the Conservative Party's attachment to the federalist EPP group has diluted our principles without furthering our aims.

EU projects in Britain are exposed as the worst deals in history, costing us £2 towards the European budget for every £1 we get back.

The case against British membership of the euro is covered in full, and this of course is the next battleground. Politicians hold in trust the rights of the electorate to choose, and to choose not just once but regularly and repeatedly. If Britain gives up the pound we will permanently transfer decisions about our economy and government away from people who are elected and can be removed, to people who are not elected and cannot be removed. That is why it is at root a political decision and has little to do with Gordon Brown's five self-serving economic tests.

This collection of articles and speeches is excellent ammunition in the coming struggle and I commend it.

The Rt. Hon. David Heathcoat-Amory MP
18 January 2002

Acknowledgements

This book would never have been possible without the efforts of thousands of Conservatives across the East Midlands, who worked so hard to secure an excellent result in the 1999 European parliament elections, and without whose help I should never have become an MEP. Equally, I am grateful to all those who have invited me to their events up and down the region and given me the opportunity to tell them a little of what is being done in their name in Brussels.

My previous Press Officer Sally McNamara in Nottingham (where she is a Conservative City Councillor) worked for Chris Heaton-Harris and me, and has done a marvellous job. She has placed most of the articles which make up this book in regional newspapers.

I should like to thank my staff past and present who have helped in many ways, including my previous research assistant Hannah Ladkin, and *stagière* Amber Bielecka, in her gap year after leaving Rugby School, who sorted out the archive.

Thanks also to my wife Sara, who tolerates me doing a job which requires me to be away from home four days a week, and then away again, around the region, for most of the remaining three days.

Finally, I should like to express my appreciation of the English countryside in Leicestershire, where I love to walk the greyhound in my rare spare moments. The nation-state is a wonderful but abstract concept. Somehow the grass and trees, the fields and hedgerows, the churches and farmhouses around my village clothe the abstraction with reality, and I can say with Sir Walter Scott "This is mine own, my native land".

Roger Helmer
Brussels, February 2002

Roger Helmer MEP

Member of the Industry, External Trade, Research and Energy Committee
Substitute Member of the Employment and Social Affairs Committee
Substitute Member of the Regional Policy, Transport and Tourism Committee
Member of the pro Country Sports Intergroup F.A.C.E
Member of the Textiles Intergroup
Member of the SOS Democracy Intergroup

Brussels
European Parliament, ASP 14E 242, rue Wiertz, B-1047. Brussels

Brussels Research Assistant - Sally McNamara
Tel: 00 32 2 284 7764
Fax: 00 32 2 284 9764
e-mail: rhelmer@europarl.eu.int
website: www.rogerhelmer.org.uk

Strasbourg
European Parliament, Allée du Printemps, BP 1024/F, F-67070, Strasbourg
Cedex
Tel: 00 33 3 81 77764
Fax: 00 33 3 81 79764

Constituency
Blaby Conservative Association, 35 Lutterworth Road, Blaby, Leicester. LE8
4DW
Tel: 00 44 116 277 9992
Fax: 00 44 116 278 6664
e-mail: rogerhelmer@tory.org

Press Officer - Zoë Aylward
Conservative Headquarters, King Edward Court, King Edward Street,
Nottingham. NG1 1EW
Tel: 00 44 115 941 5328   Fax: 00 44 115 941 5329

About the Author

Roger Helmer was born in London in 1944, the son of a university lecturer, and was educated at Kind Edward VI School in Southampton. In 1962 he took a State Scholarship to Churchill College, Cambridge, where he studied mathematics, graduating in 1965. Initially joining Procter & Gamble in Newcastle on Tyne, he made a career in international marketing and general management, with several multinational companies including National Semiconductor, Readers' Digest, Tootal Group/Coats Viyella and United Distillers/Guinness PLC/Diageo.

He has worked in Europe, America, East and South East Asia, with extended periods of residence in Hong Kong, Thailand, Singapore, Malaysia and Korea (where he was Vice President of the British Chamber of Commerce). In 1988 he established a new joint-venture business for Tootal in Saigon, Vietnam.

In September 1998, following his selection as #1 Euro-candidate for the Conservatives in the East Midlands, he gave up his day job as Managing Director of a textile company in Leicester, to campaign full-time.

He was a Vice President of CAFE, Conservatives Against a Federal Europe, and is on the advisory board of the European Journal, which has published several of his articles (some included here).

In 1967 he married Veronica Logan, whom he met at Procter & Gamble. They had two children, Stuart (1974) and Victoria (1975). His first marriage ended in 1984, and in 1987 he married Sara Thomas (*née* Winterbottom). She has one son, Duncan (1970). Roger Helmer lives with his wife, several horses, two cats and a greyhound, in rural Leicestershire.

Introduction

British prosperity, democracy, and even security are under increasing threat from European integration, as more and more powers are passed from our elected representatives to unelected and unaccountable institutions in Brussels, and to activist judges who use the European "human rights" agenda, the convention and charter, to create new legislation through precedent and case law.

I decided to stand for the European parliament in 1999 because I wanted a platform to oppose the European integration project. The Conservatives won the 1999 European election, in the sense that we achieved a higher share of the vote, and more MEPs, than Labour. I find that as a consequence some constituents think we are in a position to call the shots in the parliament. Sadly, this is not the case.

Even the EPP/ED political group to which we are attached (see Chapter 4) has only 232 members out of the parliament's total complement of 626. And we Conservatives are only 35 — about 15% of the EPP's 232 members. On left-right issues we frequently lose the votes, while on federalist issues we almost always lose.

We are sometimes able to knock the rough edges off bad legislation, but we cannot turn the project around. We will only sort out Britain's problem with Europe when we have a Conservative government in Westminster committed to renegotiation of the treaties. So in my view, the most important task for Conservative MEPs is to work to support the party, and to alert the British people to what is being done in their name. This is why, early in 2000, I published a book of collected speeches and press articles entitled "Straight Talking on Europe".

Since then, a lot more water has flowed under the bridge, and a lot more bad legislation has come out of Brussels. I have continued to be very active in the East Midlands region, in speeches and in the media, so this new book is a reflection of the work I have done since the last one.

Unlike "Straight Talking", I have organised the material in this book into chapters under broad subject headings. This means that in some cases succeeding pieces may repeat some of the key points from earlier pieces, but generally I have tried to select material to avoid unnecessary repetition. Where repetition occurs, my excuse is that some points are worth extra emphasis!

The title may seem a little presumptuous. But unless we start to make a clear stand for our country's independence, our future as an off-shore province in the European super-state will be bleak.

Roger Helmer
Brussels, February 2002

Chapter One

Why the EU is Bad for Britain

In January 2001 I was invited to address the Democracy Movement in Matlock, Derbyshire. This was my speech.

Speech, Democracy Movement, January 19th 2001

I want to tell you about one of the great historical developments of the twentieth century. The empire builders thought they could create a super-state to rival the USA, a super-state with global reach. They thought they could subsume proud and ancient nation states into their new union. They thought they could impose their own uniform economic and social policies over a vast area. They thought they could ride roughshod over the opinions and the instincts of the people.

I am speaking, of course, of the Soviet Union, but you could be forgiven for thinking I meant the European Union. We should not push the parallels too far, but they are clear for all to see. Take the Common Agricultural Policy, which is perhaps the last surviving example of Soviet-style central planning still in captivity. We tell farmers what they can produce, and how much they can produce, and how much they will get paid.

The consequences of denying market mechanisms are clear enough. The CAP has been a disaster for the environment, as we subsidise production and incentivise the use of chemical fertilisers and pesticides. It has been a disaster for housewives, with each British family paying hundreds of pounds a year in excess food prices. And it has not done a great deal of good for farmers, who were heading for crisis even before the BSE story broke.

We talk about the need for reform, we've been tinkering at the margins for twenty-five years, yet nothing really changes.

But the CAP is only an extreme example of a phenomenon we see in so many of the projects and programmes and plans of the EU. They do things that no sane person could justify, that no-one could defend, and yet which no-one can change. On a smaller scale, consider the daft charade of the European parliament commuting from Brussels to Strasbourg once a month. Facilities are duplicated. The new Strasbourg parliament cost £300m. It is

1

not just the MEPs, but the whole circus, who travel to and fro. Bureaucrats, officials, drivers, medical staff, even the man who advises your assistant on her pension. Plus trucks and wagon loads of paper and equipment, every month.

The process costs the European tax-payer around £90m a year. Entirely pointless and wasteful, yet we can do nothing about it.

The problem comes down in the end to democratic accountability. Virtually every one involved in the European process agrees that there is a "democratic deficit" in the EU. Indeed my former colleague the turncoat MEP Bill Newton Dunn claims to have invented the phrase. But what solution do they propose? More powers for the European parliament! Just give us more powers, perhaps have an elected Commission, and we will have a perfect, democratically accountable EU.

I never believed this was possible, and after eighteen months as an MEP I am even more sceptical. Let me quote two great political philosophers to you.

In the nineteenth century John Stuart Mill said *"Where a people lack fellow feeling, and **especially when they read and speak different languages**, the common public opinion necessary to representative government cannot exist"*. He could have been describing the EU.

And in the twentieth century, Enoch Powell said much the same. Pointing out the very word democracy comes from the Greek *demos*, a people, he said that for democracy to work, the people need to share enough in common, in terms of culture, history, language and economic interests that they are prepared to accept governance at each other's hands. Clearly, the nation state meets those criteria. Clearly, the EU does not.

I am prepared to accept a decision made by British MPs at Westminster, even if I disagree with it. But I am not prepared to accept a decision made by a coalition of Portuguese and Greeks and Lithuanians, and there is no earthly reason why I should. It lacks any democratic legitimacy.

Nor do the institutional structures of the EU allow accountability. We have a vast structure of Byzantine complexity, with five major institutions, the Commission, the Council, the Central Bank, the Parliament, the Court of Justice, with only one, the parliament, making even a pretence of democratic legitimacy. Even there, the processes of proportional representation mean an endless round of horse-trading and compromise. You may have heard the definition of EU horse-trading: I agree to do something bad for my country in exchange for the other guy agreeing to do something bad for his country.

2

There's the old metaphor of turning the super-tanker around. Imagine that super-tanker with 626 MEPs on the bridge, all pulling the wheel different ways, and you can see why it's so difficult to achieve change. It's a case of institutional inertia and corporate constipation.

The European parliament is driven by the officials, and we MEPs struggle to make an impression. We fly back and forth, and get fired at elections, but the officials are always there. One of the ways they control the agenda is by the sheer volume of legislation, pumped out faster than we can read it or understand it. One of my senior colleagues recently remarked that if all the MEPs went away, the Parliament would keep right on going.

Right from the start, the EU has been an élitist project, driven by visionary leaders dragging a reluctant and sceptical public behind them. Jean Monnet, one of Europe's founding fathers, is on record as saying "If we had told the people of Europe what we intended to do, they would never have let us do it". A sad parallel with Edward Heath, who would not have got Britain into the EU if he had been honest about his objectives.

They tell us, of course, that there is no intention to build a super-state — even while we see it being assembled before our eyes. The EU has a flag, an anthem, a passport. It has a parliament and a central bank. It has a common monetary policy, and is working on common taxation. It has a common foreign and security policy. It is working on common diplomatic representation, a common justice system, a European Army. It either has, or is putting in place, all the attributes of a single state. If it looks like a duck, and walks like a duck, and quacks like a duck, it probably is a duck.

Most worrying of all, it now has the so-called Charter of Fundamental Rights, which taken with the treaties amounts to a constitution for the state of Europe. And despite the reassuring name, it is a profoundly illiberal charter. In Article 52, it provides that human rights can be suspended in the interests of the Union. No safeguards. The EU is judge and jury in its own cause.

It is another sinister parallel with the USSR. Constitutional lawyers in the old Eastern European states would have been proud of it — the so-called *"raison d'état"*. As my colleague Dan Hannan has remarked, the ability to suspend its own constitution is the defining characteristic of a tyranny. Hitler's Nazi constitution had just such a clause.

In Britain, our rights are not dependent on charters, or politicians, or governments, or institutions. They derive from the centuries-long evolution of our democracy and common law. But now the EU comes along and says, not only that our rights come from Europe, but they are merely borrowed, and can be taken away at any time.

Now the Europhiles are constantly telling us that the nightmare of the Euro-state is unreal. Would the French or the Germans be prepared to give up their national identity, they ask? Are the French any less French because of the EU? Frederick Forsyth gives a typically robust answer to that question. Were the French any less French in 1942 than in 1938? Of course not. They still ate garlic and bought baguettes in the morning. The difference was that in 1938 they ruled themselves, while in 1942 they were ruled by Germany.

If we allow ourselves to be submerged finally in the Euro-state, we will still be allowed Maypoles and Morris dancing. But we shall have abandoned democracy and self-determination. We shall have lost the right to manage our own affairs.

All around the world people are fighting for independence and self-determination. Robin Cook sends British troops to Sierra Leone to support freedom and democracy in that country. Yet when we in Britain stand up for independence and democracy, we are made to feel guilty about it!

Let me finally turn to the question of the Euro, because that represents the Rubicon which we would cross if we were to join. There are powerful economic arguments against joining, which I don't have time to address in detail tonight — may I put in a plug for my book which is available here tonight, and which makes the case thoroughly?

But the remarkable thing about the Euro is that only in Britain is it sold on economic grounds. Everyone in Europe recognises that it is primarily a political project, with the clear objective of political union.

A country that loses control of its monetary policy and its currency, and inevitably therefore of its taxation, is no longer an independent nation. It has become a mere province in a larger state.

The Europhiles are fond of telling us that more than half our trade is with the Euro-zone — although the true figure is a little less than half. They never tell us that three quarters of our enormous global investments are outside the Euro-zone, and primarily in dollars. They don't tell us that most of our non-Sterling trade settlements are in dollars, and that therefore the dollar is a much more important currency for the UK than the Euro.

They told us that inward investment would suffer. But in 1999, the first year of the Euro and the latest year for which inward investment data are available, FDI in Euro-land went down by 2%, while in the three non-Euro EU states, it went up by a whacking 66%. The UK got the lion's share, and even little Sweden got more FDI than France or Germany!

4

They bang on about Japanese investment. But a recent research study shows a sixth of Japanese senior managers believe Britain should join the Euro, a sixth think we should not, and the other two thirds don't care one way or the other. They talk up the bad news for the car industry at Ford and Vauxhall, but they don't mention the new production at Honda in Swindon and Toyota in Derby. Of course there is serious restructuring in the car industry, but the industry expects that more cars will be built in Britain in five years' time than today.

A recent report shows that only one country in the EU has a significant majority of public opinion behind the Euro project — and that's the Grand Duchy of Luxembourg! Yet they press on — another example of the Eurocrats' contempt for public opinion.

The UK is the world's fourth largest economy, with the world's fourth largest currency, and is the world's second largest global investor. If relatively small economies like Switzerland and Singapore and Canada can prosper with their own currencies, it is just plain daft to suggest that Britain needs to join a larger currency bloc. But if we did — I stress *IF* — it would make more sense to join the dollar than the Euro.

I was elected to the European parliament as a Conservative, and we Conservatives believe that European integration has gone quite far enough, and too far in key areas. We want to repatriate the CFP. We want radical changes to the CAP. We want genuine flexibility, that works both ways — not, as the EU means flexibility, simply a ticket to faster integration. We believe that the essence of the EU is free trade in a Single Market, interpreted narrowly — in other words, the Common Market that we thought we were voting for in 1975.

Our opponents say that these objectives are unrealistic. But I am convinced that if we make our partners understand that we will have membership on our terms or not at all, they will do what they have to do to keep us on board. This, at any rate, is what we are resolved to do. ❧❧❧

Back in May 2000, I was invited to join a debate with Nick Clegg, the Lib-Dem MEP for the East Midlands. While it covered some similar ground, it also took some different approaches:

Speech for Euro-debate

Ladies and Gentlemen, I stand before you tonight as a committed pro-European. Forty years ago, in my grammar school debating society in

Southampton, I moved the motion that Britain should join the Common Market. Twenty-five years ago, I voted YES in the referendum to remain in the Common Market. I took that view because I believe in free trade, I believe in co-operation between independent democracies, and I wanted the UK to have access to the European market.

So if by "Europe", you mean the diverse nations and peoples and cultures of Europe, if you mean trade and co-operation between independent, sovereign nation states on this continent, then I am as pro-European as anyone in this room tonight.

However, the word Europe has in recent decades taken on a darker meaning. It means the European Union. It means a structure of institutions which are profoundly anti-democratic. It means decision-making by unelected and unaccountable bureaucrats. It means the leaching away of power from Westminster to Brussels. It may yet mean the creation of a single state of Europe, and the end of centuries of British independence and democracy. If that is what we mean by Europe, then I am absolutely and passionately opposed to it.

Nations enter into treaties for their own benefit and self-interest, and those treaties must be monitored to ensure that the benefits which were envisaged are actually delivered. So why did we join the Common Market? The argument was a simple one of economic advantage. In the early '70s, tariffs on industrial goods were typically 30 to 40%, creating a huge handicap for Britain's trade with the continent. But since then, through the good offices of GATT and the WTO, tariffs are down to 3 or 4%, so nine tenths of our reason for joining has gone away.

Meantime the growing tide of European regulation has started to place huge burdens on British industry, and to reduce our productivity and competitiveness. This malevolent process is not over – indeed it is gaining speed. There is huge pressure for tax harmonisation in Europe, which would be a body-blow to the British economy.

The direct cost of our EU membership, net of the funds we get back from the EU, amounts to around £3 billion a year. But this is only a fraction of the story. The Institute of Directors has recently published a report "EU membership – what's the bottom line?". The conclusion of their economists is that when we add in the additional costs of the CAP and regulation, membership is costing between £15 and £25 billion per year. That's roughly £1000 for every family in the country.

What are we getting for our money? There are those who argue that, expensive and frustrating as it is, EU membership is the price we pay for peace in

Europe. But of course this is a nonsense. It is NATO, not the EU, that underwrites European security. Indeed with the anti-American undercurrents in some member states, and proposals to create a European army, it could be argued that the EU is increasing, not reducing, the risk of another major war. Then there is the argument, put forward by the pressure group "Britain in Europe", that "Cut off from Europe, 3 million jobs face the axe". This must surely be the most dishonest and mendacious claim ever made in British politics. It may be that 3 million jobs depend on trade with Europe, but they would only be at risk if we were to stop trading with Europe. There is not a single politician in the UK proposing that we should discontinue such trade. Britain in Europe seems to have forgotten that millions of jobs in the US, in China, in Japan also depend on trade with Europe. But they don't depend on EU membership, and still less do they depend on those countries joining the Euro. US trade with the EU is growing faster than Britain's trade with our partners.

There is the argument that **inward investment** depends on the EU. But all the research amongst inward investors shows they come for our enterprise culture, limited regulation, low taxes, and of course the English language. If inward investors were looking for Euro-zone membership, they have eleven countries to choose from. But in fact they come here, to Britain, in great and growing numbers. The threat to inward investment is not that we are outside the Euro-zone – it is that we are importing European social regulation, and taking on the competitive disadvantages of our continental partners.

Robin Cook tells us that 60% of our trade is with Europe, but Robin Cook is wrong. The true figure is well below 50%, and it is declining – because growth is faster in the rest of the world than in Europe's sclerotic economies. Euro-luvvies like to quote the trade figure, but there are other figures they mention less often. Did they ever tell you that Britain is the world's second largest global investor (after the USA), and that three-quarters of our investments are outside the Euro-zone? Did they tell you that three quarters of inward investment to the UK is from outside the Euro-zone? Did they tell you that the UK is the largest inward investor into the USA, and that the USA is the largest inward investor into the UK? Did they tell you that of all Britain's trade conducted in foreign currencies, the majority is denominated in US dollars? The hell they did!

I'd like to let you in to a secret. Britain is not a European economy at all. It is an Atlantic economy. On key measures like patterns of trade, oil production, interest-rate dependence, demographics, we are far more like America than like Europe. Our currency is relatively stable against the dollar, volatile against European currencies. Our business cycle correlates positively with New York, negatively with Frankfurt.

This then is the background to the great Euro debate. I usually reckon that it takes half an hour to make the economic and constitutional case against the Euro, and for those who want it in more detail, my book is on sale at the back of the hall! I will try to be brief.

The Euro has lost 25% of its value against the dollar in the seventeen months since launch. This reflects the assessment by global financial markets of economic prospects in the world's most over-governed, over-regulated, over taxed and over-borrowed economic area. It is a dramatic fall, and will have serious consequences for the whole Euro-zone. But this is not the key argument against the Euro. Currencies fluctuate. In due course, even the Euro may recover.

The fundamental case against the Euro is that it imposes the same interest rates and monetary policy on widely divergent economies. Monetary policy is a vital tool of economic management. It is essential to prevent boom-and-bust and to promote healthy, non-inflationary growth. A one-size-fits-all interest rate will be wrong for most countries, most of the time. We should be throwing away the most important tool of economic management. It would be like trying to drive a car with the steering lock on.

Fortunately, you don't need to take my word for it. We have what in my former profession I should have called a test-market. There is one other member state whose economy, like Britain's, is closely linked with the US – another Atlantic economy. Ireland, like us, enjoys massive investment from the US. Like us, its economy moves more with New York than with Frankfurt. But it opted to join the Euro – in the mistaken belief that we would soon follow. Of course the UK is Ireland's biggest trading partner, and they might have done better to join Sterling than the Euro.

So what has happened in Ireland? With big injections of EU funds and US investment, the economy was already on a roll, with interest rates at 6 to 7%. Then they joined the Euro, and interest rates halved. Reported inflation in Ireland is now the highest in the EU at 5%+. Retail purchases, car sales, house prices are running out of control. A carefully crafted wages pact is now under great pressure and will soon fail. Ireland has a classic bubble building up, but has given away the means to control it. A hard landing will follow. This is exactly what would have happened here if Britain had joined the Euro in January 1999.

I must give credit to Nick Clegg for coming here tonight to speak in favour of the Euro. He is only the second politician in two years who has been prepared to come out and debate the issue with me. But the bad news, Nick, is that the national debate is over, and the Euro has lost.

No doubt Nick will point out the problems caused for British exporters by the weak Euro (and remember it is a weak Euro, not a strong Pound), although we should remember that in recent years both Germany and Japan have learned to live successfully with strong currencies, and have been proud of them.

The Liberal solution is simple. All the government has to do is to announce a date for joining the Euro, and suddenly, as if by magic, down will come the exchange rate and interest rates and everything in the garden will be lovely. They've even suggested that Gordon Brown should invest £22 billion from the mobile phone auctions in the Euro, to help bolster it.

As you might expect from the Liberal party, this is pure Alice-in-Wonderland economics. If the last twenty years have taught us anything, it is that government statements are powerless to change the value of currencies, and that "investing" in a failing currency is just throwing good money after bad. The only way to talk up the Euro is to go for massive deregulation and tax cuts in Euro-land to promote growth and to suck in investment, but there is no sign of Euro-land countries grasping the nettle.

So which way forward for Britain in Europe? We've seen the massive risks to our prosperity posed by the Euro. We've discussed the massive, on-going and increasing costs of EU membership. As politicians, we cannot expect the British people to accept these huge burdens forever. Already a third of the British people favour leaving the EU. Unless we can resolve the position in our favour, the demands for withdrawal will become irresistible.

William Hague has said that the essential element in EU membership is acceptance of "the rights and responsibilities of the Single Market". The current Inter Governmental Conference is discussing what they call "flexibility", which means in Brussels-speak a right for sub-groups of member states to integrate faster, so help us. I say YES to flexibility, but I say that it must work both ways. Flexibility for more integration for those who want it, flexibility for others to opt-out of all except strictly Single Market issues. Opt-outs would include economic and monetary policy, social, industrial and employment policy, the common foreign and security policy, home affairs and *corpus juris*, and of course fisheries and agriculture.

I shall be urging the Conservative Party to commit itself in its next general election manifesto to a radical renegotiation of the treaties, which would leave the EU looking, at least from the British perspective, like a free trade area. Now Nick will say that treaty changes require unanimity, and we won't get it. That of course is what they said to Maggie Thatcher when she went to negotiate the rebate.

Certainly it will be a tough negotiation, but our ace-in-the-hole must be a clear understanding that either we get the terms we want, or the whole question of continued membership will arise. We will have membership on our terms, or not at all. There are well-established precedents for countries outside the EU to have free-trade agreements with it – Norway, Switzerland, Mexico – and while Conservative policy is to stay in the EU, many of us feel that withdrawal would be preferable to the status quo.

No doubt Nick will argue that calls for renegotiation are merely code for withdrawal. But even he will agree that if I have a reputation for anything in the European Parliament, it is for straight talking. When I call for renegotiation, that's exactly what I mean. Withdrawal is only a fall-back position if renegotiation fails.

If Tony Blair were here – and looking round, I don't think he is – he would be calling my position "extremist". Millbank's strategy for the general election is to dub Conservative politicians extremist. They even have a target list of Tory Eurosceptics, and I assume I am on it, since Tony Blair recently quoted me at Prime Minister's questions in the House of Commons.

If it's extremist to believe that the British people have the right and the capability to govern themselves, if it's extremist to prefer democracy to centralisation and statism, if it's extremist to believe that the world's fourth largest economy can prosper with its own currency, if it's extremist to believe in the independence and sovereignty of this nation, then I'm proud to be an extremist, and I invite you all to be extremists with me. ❧❧❧

In November 2001 I contributed an article to a publication called "Public Service Review":

The EU: Solution, or Problem?

Last October a heavy volume thudded onto my desk: it was called "Public Service Review: European Union".

Glancing through, it seemed to be pure federalist propaganda. It started with a foreword by the European Parliament (EP) president, Nicole Fontaine, criticising the Nice Treaty for being insufficiently federalist and integrationist. (I have been following the career of Nicole Fontaine as President of the parliament. Although a member of the so-called "centre-right" EPP political group in the parliament, many of her speeches have seemed downright Old Labour).

It was followed by a piece by the discredited President of the Commission, Romano Prodi, praising the Treaty of Nice and criticising the people of Ireland for exercising their democratic rights by voting against the ratification of the Treaty.

Then a piece by the arch-federalist Belgian Prime Minister Guy Verhofstadt, currently President-in-Office of the Council under the EU's rotating presidency (I write in November 2001). I recently met Verhofstadt with a group of Euro-realist MEPs to appeal for proper representation of our views at the proposed "Convention" ahead of the 2004 IGC — he offered to "put our request on the table". It has often been pointed out that Belgium is the greatest enthusiast for integration, not only because the EU institutions are located in Brussels, but because Belgium is scarcely a nation-state to start with.

Next comes Graham Watson MEP, leader of the pro-federalist British Lib-Dem group in the EP. (A recent study by Dr. Simon Hix of the LSE on MEPs' voting records since 1999 showed the British Lib-Dems as the most leftist and federalist national delegation in the Liberal group in the EP). He extols the incipient European justice system which is set to overturn rights and freedoms which Englishmen and women have enjoyed since Magna Carta.

I could go on, but you get my drift. Admittedly there is a piece by my colleague Jonathan Evans MEP, calling into question some technical problems with European competition law (p88), and another by the highly respected Chairman of the EP's Environment Committee, Caroline Jackson MEP (p117), calling for the EU to do less and do it better, but the overwhelming thrust of the publication is a paean of praise for the EU and all its works.

Madame Fontaine says, with a straight face, that "our citizens want to see the Union develop a genuine *communautaire* approach". What evidence is there for such a wild claim? In 1992 the Danes voted against Maastricht, and were told to vote again until they got the right answer (a classic example of "biased finality"). The French people approved Maastricht by such a tiny margin that France has never dared to hold another referendum on a European issue.

Only this year the Swiss voted three-to-one against commencing accession negotiations. The Danes voted against the Euro. The Irish famously voted against the Treaty of Nice. Opinion polls show 60% of Germans opposed to the single currency — but no-one offered them a referendum. A reasonable man might conclude that public opinion was at most fairly balanced on the European project, perhaps a little against. No demand for a *communautaire* approach there.

Shocked at the flagrant bias and propaganda of the book, I immediately 'phoned Simon Adderley, commissioning editor, to protest, and to ask who had funded it. I naturally assumed that this was a piece of EU-funded propaganda, and was astonished to hear that it was a commercial publication funded by advertising. I am amazed that the public would want to read such stuff, or that advertisers would see fit to support it. But a word in Mr. Adderley's favour. He recognised my criticism of pro-integrationist bias, and invited me to draft a response. This is it.

In my view, the European project is the greatest single threat to our prosperity, our democracy, and now increasingly to our security (with the possible exception of international terrorism). A bold statement. Let me justify it.

Before my election to the EP in 1999, I spent over thirty years in general management rôles in major multinational companies, in Britain, Europe and Asia. Since my selection in 1998, I have visited literally hundreds of businesses, large and small, across my East Midlands region. Overwhelmingly the biggest single complaint from business is the suffocating weight of EU regulation. The European social model is destroying our competitiveness.

In a single week, at our last Plenary session in Strasbourg, we passed the Hautala report, full of politically correct nonsense and gender-mainstreaming, which will place new recording and reporting obligations on businesses across Europe. The Ghilardoti report, which will impose a rigid German-style industrial relations régime, and give trade unions an effective veto over management decisions. And the ruinous report by Thorning Schmidt (the Kinnocks' daughter-in-law — the Kinnocks have turned the EU into a family business), the Physical Agents (Vibration) Directive, which threatens to limit HGV drivers to six hours' work a day — and tractor drivers to two hours!

We hear a lot about the "self-evident benefits" of EU membership. Yet an independent report commissioned by the Institute of Directors shows that our membership is costing a **net** £15 to £25 billion a year, which could be set to double as tax harmonisation takes hold. And even the pro-federalist Economist magazine (20/10/2001) favourably reviews a paper by Hindley and Howe which concludes that British withdrawal from the EU would be broadly neutral in economic terms.

The Single Currency also threatens our prosperity. By applying a single interest rate across Europe, we shall have the **wrong** rate for most countries, most of the time, leading to demand cycle instability — boom and bust — recession and business failures. The looming demographic/pensions crisis in continental Europe means that a vote for the Euro is a vote for higher taxes, higher interest rates, higher unemployment.

And the EU damages our democracy. Slice by stealthy slice, our ability to govern ourselves is being passed to unelected and unaccountable officials in Brussels. A Bow Group paper by my colleague Nirj Deva MEP shows how 55% of new legislation affecting the UK now comes from Brussels, often with precious little scrutiny in Westminster. This would increase, he argues, to 75% if we joined the Euro, and 85% with tax harmonisation.

A Centre for Policy Studies paper by Theresa Villiers MEP shows how tax harmonisation is not some remote threat, but is happening *now*, and costing jobs *now*, as the Commission constructs procedural devices to by-pass the national veto.
Some imagine that a little tweaking could make the EU institutions "democratic". But there are two reasons why this cannot happen. First, the Byzantine complexity of the institutions denies accountability and trans-parency. But even if this were corrected, meaningful representative democracy simply cannot work across such diverse nations. As political philosophers from John Stuart Mill to Roger Scruton have pointed out, democracy requires a *demos,* a people, with sufficient in common, in terms of history, culture, language and economic interests that they are prepared to accept majority decisions even when they disagree with them. This condition is met in the nation state. It simply cannot be achieved in the EU 15, much less a future enlarged EU of say 27 members.

And the EU threatens our security. Despite vague claims that "Europe has kept the peace", the truth is that NATO and the transatlantic alliance are our only guarantee of security. Far from underlining the need for a Common European Security and Defence Policy (as Nicole Fontaine has argued), the recent terrorist outrages have thrown the transatlantic alliance into sharp focus, and shown up European defence initiatives for what they are — a political charade animated by latent anti-Americanism.

When the chips are down, the USA is Britain's most reliable ally — and *vice versa.*

There is a real danger that the creation of EU defence structures — big on rhetoric, pathetically under-resourced in men and equipment — will encourage the USA to disengage from Europe. There is even a real longer-term danger of setting up damaging transatlantic rivalry — surely the last thing we want.

So there you have it. Estimates of the economic value of EU membership vary from zero to negative, while our democracy and security are under threat. We have a choice. Britain can pursue its manifest destiny as a global trading nation — the world's fourth largest economy and second largest global investor — or it can opt for a future as an offshore province in an inward-looking, protectionist, old-fashioned regional bloc.

Let's choose freedom, democracy, prosperity, independence and self-determination. ❧❧❧

References:

"Who Governs Britain?", Nirj Deva MEP, Bow Publications Ltd., 0207 431 6400, www.bowgroup.org

"European Tax Harmonisation: The Impending Threat" Theresa Villiers MEP, Centre for Policy Studies, 0207 222 4488, mail@cps.org.uk, www.cps.org.uk
"EU Membership:What's the Bottom Line?" Graeme Leach, Institute of Directors, March 2000

"Better Off Out?", Brian Hindley & Martin Howe, Institute of Economic Affairs

Early in 2000 I attended the EPP/ED group's "Study Days" in Paris. All recognised political groups in the parliament have such sessions twice a year, and they rotate between member states. They are a waste of tax-payers' money. We might just as well have our meetings in Brussels, much more cheaply. But like so much that happens in the EU, most people can see that it's a bad idea, but no-one can change it. The requirement to visit the member states is written into the treaties.

Nevertheless, I was determined to take the opportunity to ensure that our partners in the EPP knew exactly where we Conservatives stood on the issues.

Speech at the EPP Conference in Paris, March 8th 2000

I have carefully studied the IGC (Nice Treaty) proposals. They are totally integrationist and designed to undermine the nation state, and they are totally unacceptable. Let me be very clear. This is not an issue of nuance or interpretation. This is not a question of timing. This is not just a couple of difficult points where we might reach a compromise. The whole thing is wrong from start to finish, and we want no part of it.

In the last hundred years, the British people have fought major wars to defend their independence and their democracy. We have twice faced continental powers who sought to make our country a mere province in a greater European entity. Now, for the third time, we face the same threat. This time, thank God, the weapons are made not of hard steel and high explosive, but of soft words and mendacious treaties. But the objectives are the same. The aims are the same. And our response will be the same.

This is why Tory leader William Hague says that now we face the greatest threat to British independence for fifty years.

Now I know that one or two of my colleagues are dazzled by the European dream. And they are no doubt itching right now to get up on their feet and contradict me. So it is important to tell you that the view I have set out is shared by the majority of the British people, by a great majority of Conservative members and activists, and by a great majority of Conservative MPs at Westminster.
A recent poll showed that 69% of British people oppose EMU and more than a third want to leave the EU altogether. If you insist on dragging us, kicking and screaming, down the integrationist road, the demand for withdrawal will become unstoppable – and you will have only yourselves to blame.

In conclusion, let me be completely and absolutely clear. Let me leave no possible room for doubt. The British people have had enough of European integration. We will have no more of it. The next Conservative government will not only call a halt to integration, but is committed to rolling it back in key areas, for example in fisheries. We therefore reject these IGC proposals in total. We reject them root and branch. We reject them from start to finish.

Madam Chairman, the gloves are off. This is a bare-knuckle fight for British independence and sovereignty. ❧❧❧❧

An article for my monthly newsletter in January 2000 also illustrated the dangers Britain faces in the EU — this time over European horse-trading

European Blackmail

There's a regular ding-dong going on in the EU over the so-called withholding tax. Tony Blair found himself isolated on the issue in Helsinki. This tax would cause huge damage and job losses in the City (with knock-on effects for the whole UK economy) , and would hurt financial markets across the EU. Billions of pounds of Euro-bond business would go outside the EU altogether, to Switzerland and the USA. So far, Gordon Brown has stood firm against it (although Robin Cook is starting to look wobbly).

The latest rumour in the European parliament suggests that the French and Germans are planning to sand-bag us on the issue. Regardless of the law or the rights and wrongs of the case, they are saying that unless we roll over on the withholding tax, they will (A) keep British beef out indefinitely, and (B) hold up proposals for a single market in financial services.

Now the single market in financial services is one of the very few good things that the EU is doing. It will be great not only for British fund managers, but also for investors and for industry, and it will help deal with the frightening problems facing continental state pension schemes. It's a win-win deal. But France and Germany are threatening to block it – cutting off their nose to spite their face.

Our task is to make it clear that the City of London is not to be horse-traded away. Gordon Brown must tell our partners that we will not have tax harmonisation at any price. For our sake and theirs, we must stand firm and face down our partners on the issue. And in Winston Churchill's words, we must do so "if need be, for years; if need be, alone". *✿✿✿*

A while ago the BBC ran a competition for limericks about the BBC. As the BBC is wedded to New Labour and the European project, and as I'm not sure whether BBC stands for Blair Broadcasting Corporation, or Brussels, I'm offering the following.

To challenge the Beeb who would dare?
Does the "B" stand for Brussels or Blair?
But British it is not,
Or at least not a lot,
They've sold out to the guys over there!

Chapter Two

Why the Euro is Bad for Britain

The threat of the Euro has been a constant theme in my speeches and articles. There are two important points to make. First, joining the Euro would be crossing the Rubicon into the European super-state. It would be enormously damaging and difficult to get out. But secondly, it is wrong to assume that the Euro is the only issue, and that we can rely on a referendum to throw it out. European integration is proceeding on a broad front, and there is much to worry about in addition to the Euro issue itself.

It is vitally important that we oppose British entry into the Euro, but we must remember to fight integration on other fronts as well. In April 2001 I set out my thinking on the Euro for regional papers in the East Midlands.

The Euro: Bad for the East Midlands

They told us that the Euro would be strong: it has proved to be weak. They told us it would be stable: it has been proved to be volatile. Only a few weeks ago we heard that the Euro had bottomed out. The American economy was weakening. Just give us a slide on Wall Street, they said, and funds will come rushing back to Europe, the Euro will rise, we'll see parity with the dollar or better. Well the first half of the scenario came through right on cue. A slowing US economy, swingeing falls on the Dow and the NASDAQ. But the poor old Euro just wobbled and slipped back below 90¢.

Back in 1990 we joined the ERM. All the siren voices said "Yes" — the Labour Party, the Liberals, the Tories, the TUC, the CBI. It was a disaster. Interest rates peaked at 15%, millions were thrown out of work, thousands of manufacturing companies went bankrupt, hundreds of thousands of home-owners found themselves in negative equity. It was arguably our worst financial disaster since the war.

Yet we seem to have forgotten the lesson already. If we manage our interest rates and monetary policy for the UK economy, we can achieve the Holy Grail of stable, non-inflationary growth. If we seek to manage monetary policy against external criteria, to shadow other currencies, we create disaster. The Euro is surely the triumph of hope over experience. We have finally learned which levers to pull to achieve growth and stability and high employ-ment, and now that we've found those levers, we are invited to throw them away.

Of course there are those who say that "the high Pound" is damaging East Midlands business. In fact, though, there is no high Pound — just a weak

Euro. The Pound itself has actually weakened considerably against the dollar, the world's reference currency. And joining the Euro wouldn't help — it would make matters worse. Imagine if we went to our partners today and said "Right. We'd like to join the Euro with an exchange rate of say £1 = 2.40 D Marks". They'd reply "You're welcome to join. But in the ERM (which is only suspended, not abandoned) you were in at 2.95 DM. For most of the last few years you've been well over 3 DMs. You can join at 2.95, not 2.40. That would be competitive devaluation".

OK, say the Europhiles, let's have Gordon Brown manage the exchange rate down to 2.40 DMs (they don't say how — perhaps by printing money and lowering interest rates to stoke inflation?) and then join. They forget that according to the Maastricht Treaty, we need to demonstrate stability within the ERM for two years before joining. But Gordon Brown recognises the political impossibility of re-joining the ERM.

This illustrates the Catch-22 of the Euro. We certainly shouldn't join unless we're sure we've achieved convergence, and can guarantee currency stability in the long-term. But if we can guarantee currency stability, then we don't need to join at all!

Those Europhiles who seek to justify the ERM débâcle say we entered at the wrong rate. But we can never guarantee currency stability in the long term, and that's why there can never be a "right rate" at which to join. The only right rate is the rate defined by the market on the day, and that's a variable rate. The earliest DM exchange rate I can remember from childhood, in the fifties, was 12 DMs to the pound. Imagine where we'd be now if we'd joined at that rate!

A single Europe-wide interest rate will be wrong for most countries, most of the time. Where it is too low (as currently in Ireland), there will be uncontrollable inflation. Where it is too high (Germany), growth will be slow. I hear Europhiles crowing about European growth (currently stalling) and the drop in unemployment (still much higher than the UK). They make hubristic claims about "Europe as the motor of the world economy". They never mention that this has been achieved on the back of a 25% currency devaluation.

It would be a surprise if Europe couldn't match US growth, temporarily, after such a massive devaluation. The worry must be that the growth-spurt resulting from devaluation is so modest.

Gordon Brown talks of convergence. But on the underlying drivers of our economy, convergence will not occur for decades, if ever. Our trade and massive investments are much more globalised than our partners'. We are an oil exporter. We do not have their massive state pension liabilities (which alone will drive up tax and interest rates in Euroland). We are much more sensitive to short-term interest rates. We are not a European economy at all, we are an Atlantic economy.

Finally, joining the Euro will lead to more integration, more regulation and higher taxes. The Euro is not a life-belt for East Midlands businesses. It is a ball and chain. ❧❧❧

In April 2001, I decided to write a piece challenging Gordon Brown's famous five tests — and suggesting my own alternatives!

Gordon Got It Wrong!

Gordon Brown has his famous five economic tests for British entry into the Euro – even if his Europe minister Keith Vaz can't quite remember all of them! They're all good stuff – motherhood-and-apple-pie – about stability and growth and saving jobs and financial markets. But unfortunately they're also wonderfully vague and subjective. When are they satisfied? When Gordon Brown says so, that's when! Boiled down to their essence, all Gordon's tests say is this: "It will be right to enter the Euro when it's right to enter the Euro".

What we need is some objective tests, with clear and well-defined measures, so that we can all see whether they're met or not. I'd like to offer the Chancellor my own five tests, which can be assessed on clear, pre-defined statistical criteria. Four are economic, one constitutional.

Are our trade patterns similar to our EU partners? The Euro can only succeed with convergence, which means economies must be broadly similar. Currently more than half the UK's international trade is outside Euroland. The average figure for Euroland countries is around 20%. We should not join the Euro until our figure falls within the range of the six largest EU states. Of course that means we'd have to turn off around 40% of our international trading partners, and find new ones in Euroland.

And our investment patterns? We have enormous overseas investments. We are the world's second largest overseas investor – in fact in 1999 we were the largest global investor. Three quarters of our global investments are outside Euro-land. Thus we are much more exposed to global exchange rate movements than they are. We should not join the Euro until our investment figures are within the EU range. This would mean selling off billions of pounds worth of global investments and re-investing in Euroland. Not a smart move.

Is our economic cycle convergent with Euroland? Our economic cycle is actually much closer to the US than to Euroland, because we are the largest investor in the US and the US is the largest investor in the UK, and because our trade and investment patterns are more similar to America's. There is no reason why we should converge with the EU. The same problem applies even more to Ireland, which is experiencing severe inflation problems as a result of Euro membership. Ireland, like the UK, is not a European economy. It is an Atlantic economy.

Can we guarantee long-term currency stability? Of course not. We thought we could when we joined the ERM in 1990, and we created perhaps the worst economic crisis in living memory. If we join the Euro, we have to choose a rate that will be right not for a year or ten years, but **forever.** I can remember when there were twelve D Marks to the pound: now it's about three. The only rate that can be right for decades and centuries into the future is the rate decided by the market: a floating rate. And that means keeping our own currency. This is the Catch-22 of the Euro. We shouldn't join unless we can guarantee long-term exchange rate stability. But if we **can** guarantee that stability, there's no need to join!

Do the British people agree to a future as an off-shore province of the EU super-state? This is the constitutional question. Already most of our new law comes from Brussels. If we join the Euro we will give up control over monetary policy, taxation, our economy generally. We will have signed up for the super-state, for rule from Brussels by foreign bureaucrats that we did not elect and cannot remove. This is a choice that the British people are entitled to make, but the choice must be put clearly before them in a referendum. I believe we will choose freedom and democracy.

These tests will not be satisfied in my lifetime, or in my grand-children's life-times, perhaps never. And it would be madness to sign up to the Euro if they are not satisfied. Over to you, Gordon. ❧❧❧

In September 2001 I turned to the issue that the Euro was being introduced in twelve countries without even a pretence of democratic legitimacy or approval:

An Outrage Against Democracy

In a few short months, eleven European countries will consign their historic currencies to the dustbin. The German Mark, the French Franc, the Italian Lira, the Spanish Peseta beloved of Ibiza clubbers, will disappear forever, to be replaced by Euro notes and coins. (You may be wondering why it's only eleven currencies when there are twelve Euroland countries: it's because Luxembourg uses the Belgian Franc already).

It increasingly seems that there will be a period of significant disruption in the retail and banking sectors during the changeover. We shall see.

But the astonishing thing is that this huge and portentous change will occur, this vastly risky project will be undertaken, without any real public support or enthusiasm, without even any real public acceptance. Only one country in the EU, Denmark, has had a vote on the Euro, and they voted NO.

It was a remarkable referendum. All the Danish establishment, political parties, employers, trade unions, and media, were united in calling for a YES vote, but the public took a different view. They were told that the Danish Krone would collapse, that interest rates would shoot up, that inward investment would collapse, unless they joined the Euro. All these dire predictions proved in the event to be diametrically wrong. Interest rates eased, the Krone firmed, inward investment remained strong. (In fact the three non-Euro EU countries, UK, Sweden and Denmark all do much better than the Euroland average on inward investment).

The EU Commission's own research, called "Euro-barometer", shows that there is little enthusiasm for the new currency across the EU. Only a handful of member states show a substantial margin in favour. And in Germany, for example, around 60% of people would prefer to keep the D-Mark. But they were never offered the opportunity to express a view.

Many decisions in a democracy can be made on a simple majority. As I write, we are awaiting the outcome of the Tory leadership election, and that quite rightly will be decided on a simple majority, perhaps by a small margin.

But joining the Euro is an entirely different order of decision. It carries huge potential risks. The changeover is likely to be chaotic and inflationary. The massive cost of the changeover (estimated at £36 billion in the UK alone) will never be recouped from any anticipated savings. Worst of all, loss of control over national interest rates and monetary policy may well lead to uncontrollable boom-and-bust, slower growth, higher unemployment, more bankruptcies.

Besides the economic risks, there are also huge implications for our democracy, our independence, our self-determination, our right to govern ourselves. The decision is, moreover, practically irreversible. We take the awesome responsibility of deciding not just for ourselves, but for our children and grandchildren, for all future generations.

Given the magnitude of the decision, the onus is surely on those proposing the change to make an irrefutable case, and to carry with them the overwhelming support of the people. This they have manifestly failed to do, either in Euroland or in the UK.
It would be a travesty of democracy if so great a decision were to be carried on the same basis as, say, the Welsh referendum, where only half the electorate bothered to vote and only half of those supported the measure. A great constitutional change in Wales went through on the nod of 25% of the electorate.

For so vast and dangerous a decision as scrapping the Pound, we should require a clear demonstration of wholehearted consent, with a threshold level of support — perhaps 50% of the electorate, or two thirds of those voting.

It is simply an outrage against democracy that this vast change is being carried through in Euroland without a single referendum in any Euro-land country, and with the majority opposed in the EU's largest member-state.
ༀༀༀ

In November 2001 I came across a booklet entitled "Why Mr. Blair will not win a Euro-referendum". I was impressed by the argument, and wrote a short review of the booklet.

Can Blair Pull It Off?

So far as I can see, British voters divide into two distinct groups — those who reckon that their politicians don't tell them enough about the Euro, and those who are sick to death of hearing about it. I'm hoping I can interest both groups by coming at it from a completely different angle.

Let's forget, for a moment, whether the Euro is a good thing or not (and readers who have been following these columns will have little doubt where I stand on *that!*). Let's just ask ourselves how easy it would be for Blair to win a Euro referendum — because that's what he's desperately keen to do.

Problem #1 is constructing a fair question. The government's own legislation requires the Referendum Commission to comment on the fairness and intelligibility of the question. You might think it would be easy, but it's not.

There's a lot of research that shows that people prefer to answer YES than to answer NO — regardless of the question. Consider two questions: (1) Do you want to join the Euro?, and (2) Do you want to keep the Pound? These questions are the reverse of each other. You would expect anyone who said "No" to the first, to answer "Yes" to the second. But a whole pile of research indicates that you would get more Yeses to the second question than you would get Noes to the first — just because people prefer saying YES. Market researchers call this phenomenon "Yea-saying".

Second, how much information do you include? Many people don't seem to realise that "Joining the Euro" actually means scrapping the Pound Sterling — forever.

Third, is the government allowed to include its own recommendation? Evidence indicates that this might swing the vote by several percentage points.

Even the order of the question may make a difference — people are more likely to tick the first box than the second.

Then there is the question of the exchange rate. Suppose I ask you "Do you want to sell your house?". The question is meaningless unless I tell you the price. Most of us would sell our houses for a million pounds. Not many would sell for ten thousand! There are people who say "I would agree to join the Euro at 2.40 Deutchmarks, but not at three Deutchmarks". How do they answer the question if there is no exchange rate indicated? Gordon Brown's famous Five Tests are meaningless without an exchange rate.

If we join at a high rate, we lock in a disadvantage for British industry. But if we devalue, we risk inflation, and we blow Gordon Brown's increasingly tattered reputation for prudence.

This brings us to the nub of Blair's problem. The government can't tell us the rate, because they don't decide it. Under the Maastricht Treaty, the rate is recommended by the Commission, and approved by the ECOFIN Council.

We have a veto, but Blair couldn't use it. How could he win a Euro referendum, but then come back and say to the British people "You voted for the Euro but I couldn't agree the exchange rate"? He would have zero leverage in any negotiations.

One last point. A recent study showed that when asked "Do you want to join the Euro", 54% said No and 25% Yes (the rest were don't knows). When the question added the statement "In the single currency we could no longer set our interest rates — they would be set by the European Central Bank", a whopping 69% voted No and 19% Yes. And when told that Britain's gold and foreign currency reserves would be controlled by the ECB, the Noes rose to 70% and the Yeses dropped to 16%. The more people understand the Euro, the less they like it.

For more detail, see "Why Mr. Blair will not win a Euro-referendum", by Anthony Scholefield, Futurus Publications, £3.95, Phone 0208 782 1135.

ᵶ๑ᵶ๑ᵶ๑

> *And what in hell's name is a pint?" said the barman, leaning forward with the tips of his fingers on the counter.*
> *" 'Ark at 'im! Calls 'isself a barman and don't know what a pint is! Why, a pint's the 'alf of a quart , and there's four quarts to the gallon. 'Ave to teach you the A,B,C next".*
> *"Never heard of 'em, "said the barman shortly. "Litre and half litre - that's all we serve."*
>
> *George Orwell, Nineteen Eighty-Four*

Chapter Three

The Costs of EU Membership

In March 2000 I came across a publication from the Institute of Directors, by their Chief Economist Graeme Leach. It was based on research undertaken by an independent accounting company. I was so struck by the figures on the costs of Britain's membership of the EU (which I have been quoting ever since) that I immediately wrote an article so as to share the IoD's conclusions with a wider audience.

EU Costs Every British Family £1000 a Year

How much does our British membership of the EU actually cost us? All sorts of different numbers get bandied about. The direct cost of membership, the cash difference between what we put in and what we get out, is averaging about £3 billion a year – that's Billion with a B, not million with an M. We're talking big numbers here. That's based on official Treasury figures as quoted in my previous book, "Straight Talking on Europe".

Of course we also gain considerable benefits from membership, especially from free trade in the Single Market. Against this we have to offset not only the direct costs, but also the hidden costs of the Common Agricultural policy, reckoned as several hundred pounds a year for each family. And then there's the hidden cost of excessive regulation and bureaucracy, which is imposing huge burdens on our businesses, slowing growth, and threatening jobs and prosperity. There's the desperate damage that has been done to our fishing fleet by the Common Fisheries policy.

With all these different factors, it's no wonder that its difficult for voters or politicians to see the big picture. Fortunately, the Institute of Directors has come up with a reliable answer. They've had their professional economists go through the whole thing carefully, weighing up the costs and the benefits, and they've published a report called "EU Membership – What's the Bottom Line?". The answer is shocking. They reckon that the total cost of membership – after allowing for the admitted benefits we gain – is between £15 and £25 billion a year. That's a vast sum – in round figures, a thousand pounds a year for each and every family in the land. Think what you could do with an extra thousand pounds. Think how many more schools and hospitals we could afford with £25 billion a year!

Even that huge figure is likely to get bigger as Labour signs up to more Euro-nonsense and transfers more powers to Brussels.

So should we leave the EU? The Institute of Directors says (and we in the Tory party agree with them), that we should stay and renegotiate better terms within the EU. We should ensure we keep the benefits of the Single Market, while getting out of so many other areas – social and employment policy, taxation, common foreign and security policy, immigration and asylum, fisheries policy – where the EU works against our interests.

We believe that a future Conservative government will recast our relationship with the EU so that it delivers the benefits we voted for in the 1975 referendum. And we have to make sure that those negotiations succeed. Already, a third of the British people favour complete withdrawal from the EU. Unless we can deliver better terms within the EU, the clamour for withdrawal may become irresistible. ❧❧❧

See "EU Membership — What's the Bottom Line?", by Graeme Leach, Chief Economist, Institute of Directors, March 2000. ISBN 1 901580 38 5. From Dover publications, 116 Pall Mall, London SW1Y 5ED

Another regular theme has been the threat of tax harmonisation, and the proposals to introduce entirely new Europe-wide taxes, with proceeds going directly to the Commission. I wrote in September 2001 about proposals for European infrastructure charges.

New EU Taxes!

During the First World War, we had a problem with German observation balloons. A bright young inventor came up with a neat idea. Hang a bomb on a long wire beneath a bi-plane, fly over the balloon, and blow it up. They tried it out, but in the slipstream the bomb trailed behind the plane and wouldn't hang down.

The RAF Squadron Leader helping the experiment suggested "Why don't we dispense with the line and just drop the bomb?". "Great idea" said the inventor. "And why don't we make the bomb cylindrical instead of round, and maybe give it some fins so it flies straight?". "Fantastic" said the inventor.

"So what the hell do you think those are?" shouted the Squadron Leader, pointing to the anti-balloon bombs already fitted under the wings of his plane.

Like our young inventor, the EU is brilliant at ignoring existing solutions that work well in practice, and coming up with bizarre solutions that we didn't need in the first place. Their latest wheeze is "Infrastructure charging". This means taxing all kinds of transport — including the private motorist — to reflect what they call "the real costs of infrastructure".

The excuse is environmental, but the real driving force is the passion to create new revenue streams to finance the European project.

We in the Tory Party want Europe to do less and do it better. But the empire-builders in Brussels want to do more, and to spend more of your money. They are looking at a series of new taxes to increase their so-called "own resources". Only it won't be their own resources. It will be your money.

If we want to charge motorists for their use of the road, the fairest and most efficient way is to charge duty on fuel — which we do already. In fact we in Britain pay far more than fair value for our driving. Petrol duty is cheap to collect. The EU's idea of road charging — tolls not only for motorways but for country lanes too — would be hugely expensive and disruptive to collect. Indeed the cost of collection has been estimated at around 40% of revenue (this compares to around 1% for income tax, say).

We don't want new taxes at all. Especially we don't want new European taxes, and we don't want desperately inefficient taxes. We don't want to pay twice over for our roads.

The proposed new taxes would also hit the haulage industry, trains, ports, and airports. Just as the economy seems to be facing recession, the EU comes up with a huge new tax burden which will damage industry and make Europe less competitive, and less attractive as an investment area. Trust Brussels to take a bad situation and make it worse.

Conservative MEPs will vote against these new taxes. If you are as alarmed by these proposals as I am, why don't you write to your Labour MEPs (Mel Read and Philip Whitehead)and Liberals Nick Clegg and the turncoat Bill Newton Dunn, and ask them to vote against them too. ❧❧❧

One of the joys of working in the parliament with Conservative colleagues in the European parliament is that you don't have to do all the work yourself. You can piggy-back on the work of colleagues. Theresa Villiers is a young academic lawyer who became an MEP for London in 1999. She is extraordinarily hard-working and effective. She recently produced a superbly professional and well-researched book for the Centre for Policy Studies (CPS), "European Tax Harmonisation: The Impending Threat". Again, I couldn't wait to bring it to a wider audience.

Tax Harmonisation

The EU (Like the Labour Party) says one thing and does another. After referenda in Switzerland, Denmark and Ireland they've finally realised that European integration is not flavour-of-the-month in Europe. In particular, tax harmonisation has got a bad press. So they want to call it something else. In December 1998, Oscar Lafontaine said *"Our English friends have asked us not to use the word 'harmonisation', and instead use 'co-ordination'"*.

Despite the rhetoric, the pressure for harmonised taxes goes on. My London colleague Theresa Villiers MEP has just written a book "European Tax Harmonisation: The Impending Threat", published by the Centre for Policy Studies (£7:50, CPS, 0207 222 4488). It sets out the current measures on tax in alarming detail.

The EU already has competence over VAT. It is looking at transportation and energy taxes. It is pressing for harmonisation of corporate taxes. An EU Committee headed by Britain's (Red) Dawn Primorolo is looking at ways of "preventing harmful tax competition". (Of course many economists recognise that competition in tax, as in other spheres, is never harmful, but is a thoroughly good thing).

Most ominously, the European Commission has asked Primorolo's team to extend its remit to personal income tax.

But hang on, I hear you say, don't we have a veto on tax issues? Hasn't Ken Clarke promised to keep our veto on tax (even though he agreed EU tax measures when he was Chancellor)? Well yes. And no. The Commission accepts that the tax veto is a difficulty, but has instead said it will look at "other instruments".

It has created a "Code" for corporate tax, which Gordon Brown has signed up to, and which has the same effect. It proposes to use Single Market rules (where we have no veto) when it can't get unanimity on tax. (Remember how it used Health and Safety — no veto — to push through the Working Time Directive, when we believed we had a veto under employment law?). Or it may just brow-beat us into submission as it has on taxation of the fine art market — at a cost of 5000 UK jobs.

Theresa Villiers' book is a stunning *tour-de force* — a remarkable combination of accessibility, scholarship and cogency. And it is a stark warning of the threat to our prosperity in the EU. I heartily commend it. ❧❧

Chapter Four

How the Parliament Works

In October 2000 I turned to the scandalous issue of the staffing of political groups in the European parliament.

Whose Gravy Train?

As an MEP, I am frequently asked how I am enjoying the Brussels gravy train. My usual defence is that I took a very significant salary cut in order to become an MEP, compared to my previous job as Managing Director of a Leicester company.

But I wouldn't play the violins too loudly. The generous arrangements for expenses for MEPs are open to quite proper criticism, and Tory MEPs have been leading attempts to get agreement on a new "Members' Statute" which would put expenses and allowances on a proper, transparent and defensible basis.

As you can imagine, with 626 MEPs all on widely differing national salaries, the negotiations over a new common package are exceptionally difficult, but I think there is a genuine commitment in the Parliament to get a result as soon as possible.

But if you thought that MEPs were on the gravy train, what about the Parliament staff? We have a total of over three thousand staff in the Parliament as a whole, of whom 23 are attached to our British Conservative MEP group. We have no say at all over how many staff we have – the number is determined by arcane rules within the Parliament that are extremely difficult to change.

In a sane world, we would simply be given a budget based on the number of MEPs and told to get on and hire what staff we needed. But no. We have to have an exact number of "A", "B" and "C" grades, whether we want them or not. And we don't get to hire people we want. Bizarrely, the existing staff get to draw up the short-lists.

They tell us that these people are professional civil servants, and that if they have political opinions of their own, they will put those on one side as they carry out their duties. I wish. No matter what their political views might be, they are (with a few honourable exceptions), absolutely committed to the system, to preserving their benefits, to pressing ahead with the European project. We may be offered a short list to choose from, but we can assume that every one on it is a passionate federalist. Euro-sceptics would not make first base. It is a self-selecting, self-serving oligarchy. In their eyes, the institutions are run for them. MEPs are not the elected representatives of the people, but just a temporary nuisance they have to manage.

Provided they are not caught with their hands in the till, they have more or less absolute security of tenure. Jobs for life. No effective appraisal, virtually no sacking, especially at the senior levels.

In my business career, and in quite senior positions, I never had more than a six month notice period. Why on earth should these people be given jobs for life, in addition to massive salaries and preferential tax rates?

We recently had a 27 year old appointed, reputedly on more than an MEP's salary. We have a couple of old codgers who are almost visibly coasting towards their generous pensions. They would probably be unemployable in the private sector. Yet they are both paid six figure salaries – that's Sterling, not Euros – more than double an MEP's pay!

My Tory MEP colleague Malcolm Harbour is fighting a brave action to try to reform this scandalous mess. He faces the combined opposition of the staff and the thirty or so unions who represent them. Arthur Scargill would be proud of them. We are aiming at least to get staff on to two-year rolling contracts. Not ideal, but a huge improvement.

If we push too hard, there is a danger that they may go on strike. The Parliament could be paralysed for months. And what damage would that do to the average voter? Answer: none. Most of the legislation coming out of Brussels is unnecessary, or damaging, or both. Let them strike as long as they want, I say. ❧❧❧

It's a curious paradox that a parliament elected by universal suffrage (even though turn-out in 1999 was so derisory), can be so deeply unrepresentative of the views of ordinary people. Indeed it was to represent the views of ordinary people that I put my name forward as a candidate in 1999. The following piece was penned in March 2001.

An Unrepresentative Euro-Parliament

How can the European parliament be unrepresentative? When all its members are elected by the people? Well the fact that in the UK only one person in four bothered to vote in the European elections of 1999 might

have something to do with it. But there's more to it than that.
If you visit a tennis club, you'll find that most members are wild about tennis. If you go to an angling club, you'll find most members are passionate about fishing. And if you go to the European parliament, you'll find that 85% of the members are whole-heartedly committed to the European project, to integration, harmonisation and ever-closer union. In other words, to stealing away your political choices and giving them to unaccountable Brussels bureaucrats.

That 85% figure is deeply unrepresentative. If you ask ordinary people, in Europe as well as in the UK, you'll find a wide range of attitudes to Europe. Some are enthusiasts. Some are indifferent, some apprehensive, many down-right hostile. It's difficult to put a figure on it. But in both the UK and Germany, around 65 to 70% are against the Euro (though no-one's giving the Germans a choice!). Of all member states only little Luxembourg is strongly in favour.

In the French referendum on Maastricht in 1992, the YES side won by a whisker – less than one percent. In Denmark recently, despite all the good and the great and the media, the plucky Danes voted 53 to 47% against the Euro. And of course the Swiss just voted by an overwhelming 77% against even starting to talk to the EU about membership. The peoples of Europe are certainly not 85% pro-EU.

The reason that 85% of MEPs are euro-enthusiasts is simply because, for most of the parliament's history, only euro-enthusiasts bothered to apply. The other 15% are the protest vote. Many of these are committed to a "Europe of Nations" vision. They want European countries to co-operate and to trade freely together, but to retain their independence and their own democratic governments. As so many people in the East Midlands say to me, "In the 1975 referendum we voted for free trade, a Common Market, not for political union".

We Euro-realists, from many countries, the UK, Denmark, France, Portugal, Italy, Ireland, have formed an "inter-group" – a cross-party group – dedicated to promoting our ideas. We may be few in number, but we make our voice heard. Recently we bluffed our way into the garden of the Belgian Prime Minster's residence and presented a petition for a debate on the future of the EU to the visiting Prime Minister of Sweden (Sweden currently holds the presidency of the EU).

The same "self-selection" principle that applies to MEPs also applies to the Committees of the parliament. The environment committee, for example, attracts the greenest of MEPs from all parties, which is why it is populated by earth-mothers and eco-warriors. Left to themselves, they would save the environment by destroying the economy. Of course we want a sustainable world, but we also want our grandchildren to have jobs.

In a similar way, the Employment and Social Affairs committee seems to attract leftists and trade unionists. And the Foreign Affairs Committee is full of foreigners!

Even in the Conservative Party, the European parliament used to seem a long way off, and Tory Euro-MPs ploughed their own furrow. Indeed it was because I was alarmed to hear in 1997 that they were pressing William Hague to be "more positive on the Euro" that I put my own name forward as a candidate.

In the 1999 election we saw a relatively new phenomenon – Tories putting their names forward for Europe, not because they were dazzled by the European dream, but because they were seriously worried at the damage that the EU threatened to do to our prosperity and our independence. Meantime Hague's party reorganisation ensured that the Tory MEP group started to work closely with the front-bench team at Westminster, in one seamless party.

We still have a long way to go to protect British interests and British independence, but at least we now have most of the feet pointing in the right direction. ❧❧❧

The following article appeared in a recent issue of European Journal.

Euro-realism in Brussels

The June 1999 Euro-elections were a great success for the Tories. Despite opinion polls showing a big Labour lead, the actual outcome on a low turnout gave the Tories a lead of around ten points over Labour. Tory MEP numbers were doubled from 18 to 36. It had been assumed that the new PR electoral system would favour the Tories, who were expected to be the underdogs. In fact it worked against us: the Tory share of vote was so high that on the old first-past-the-post system we would have got over fifty seats.

There was also a sharp change in the political complexion of the Tory MEP group. Up to a dozen of the new intake were committed Euro-realists, entering the European parliament not because they were dazzled by the European dream, but because they feared that the European project had gone too far.

These Euro-realist Tories were alarmed to find that they were "Associate members" of the so-called European Peoples' Party (EPP) group in the European parliament (EP), a group consisting of Christian Democrats and allies. The EPP (like Ted Heath!) is far more centrist, corporatist and interventionist than the Tory party, and is absolutely committed to the federalist project. Angela Merkel, leader of the German Christian Democrats who form the largest segment of the EPP, has said "The Christian Democrats are, and will remain, the party of European integration".

Ironically, the EPP regards itself as a centrist party, to the *left* of the Liberal group in the parliament, which is regarded as more committed to liberal economics and individualism than the EPP – a far cry from the British Lib-Dems, who nonetheless sit in the EP's Liberal group. It is easy to make the case that the closest match for the EPP amongst British parties is New Labour – although the EPP is even more blindly federalist.

The Tories' membership of the EPP, unlike most other members, is under the infamous Rule 5B, which establishes that Tories are free to follow their own manifesto when this differs from EPP policy, and in practice we have separate Tory whips on perhaps a third of plenary votes.

The new Tory MEPs fought a long rearguard action against continuing membership of the EPP, and a number came close to declaring UDI. In the end, however, a deal was struck (the "Malaga Declaration") which was supposed to create two separate groups, the EPP and the ED (=European Democrats), under a common EPP/ED umbrella. This was supposed to ensure the political integrity of the Conservative delegation while still delivering the "benefits" of being numerically the largest group in the parliament.

It soon became clear that nothing had changed. The name change from EPP to EPP/ED was purely cosmetic. Other promised changes simply failed to materialise. Euro-realists in the Tory delegation were horrified, but were unwilling to rock the boat ahead of a general election. They bided their time.

Those who favour continued Tory membership of the EPP/ED parliamentary group argue that, since everything in the EP is decided by numbers (under the so-called *d'Hondt* system), the benefits of extra clout and reach and throw-weight (pick your own metaphor!) outweigh any concerns about consistent policy. A big group would get the committee chairmanships, the *rapporteurships*, the respect which would be lost in a smaller group. Size equates to influence.

This argument scarcely bears a moment's critical examination. Indeed it is interesting to speculate why otherwise intelligent MEPs would advance it at all. Of course numbers count if everyone in the group agrees, if all the feet point the same way. But if not, if there are profound policy differences as there are between the EPP and the Tory party, membership of the larger group has *exactly the opposite effect*.

The parliament and its working committees are driven by small groups on which each recognised political group in the EP is represented. There is the Conference of Presidents, which runs the overall institution. Each of seventeen working committees has a "meeting of co-ordinators" planning the business and influencing policy.

In all these fora, the EPP speaks for the Conservatives (except on a couple of committees where the co-ordinators happen to be Tories). Far from gaining influence within the EPP, Tory views and objectives and policy simply go by default in all of these meetings. Our light is hidden under a bushel. Our voice is entirely unheard. We are "represented" by people who profoundly disagree with us on the greatest issue of the day.

The EPP recognise British Conservatives as an anti-federalist virus in their body politic, and their immune system is working full-time. They actively seek to isolate and neutralise us.

Equally, the argument that we gain committee chairmanships and *rapporteur-ships* within the EPP is belied by the success of smaller parties – the greens and the hard left – who do very nicely in the carve-up. We should do much better as 55% of a medium-sized group than as 16% of a large group.

There seems to be no basis in fact for the often-heard claim that we would get less funding outside the EPP. We have had the most appalling problems with the EPP on money and staffing issues. We have had staff foisted on us who are profoundly out of sympathy with our position. We have been forced to retain staff who should have gone long ago. Even Tory MEPs sympathetic to the EPP were so incensed by the staffing run-around that we received from it that we voted almost unanimously against a candidate proposed by the EPP.

What would happen if we were to cut the Gordian knot? There are other MEPs from other member-states who believe, as we do, in a Europe of Nations. They are bewildered and dismayed that we continue to sup with the federalists. If we Tories were to leave the EPP and run up our own flag, dozens would rally to us. We should very soon have probably the third largest group in the parliament, ahead of the Liberals, and it would be a group with common objectives, all the feet pointing forwards, all guns on the enemy.

We would be represented on all the key committees. We would hire our own staff and control our own budget We would have the satisfaction of working with like-minded colleagues. We would offer Europe a genuine alternative vision. Then we would see what clout and reach and throw-weight can really deliver.

The general election is over. Now is the time to make our move. ❧❧❧❧

A View from the South West

At a recent meeting of the British Conservative delegation in Brussels, South-West Region MEP Caroline Jackson, influential Chairman of the Environment Committee, gave her own distinctive opinion of the EPP/Tory relationship. "The EPP treats the Tories", she said, "rather as an aristocratic family treats a lunatic relative. They lock us in the West Wing and stand anxiously outside the door, waiting for the sounds of breaking furniture". ❧❧❧❧

In 2001 I finally got to grips with the financing of political groups in the European parliament. And I didn't like what I found. This article first appeared in the European Journal of July/August 2001

The Tories' Lost £½ Million

An astonishing statistic: the Conservative MEP group in the European parliament forgoes well over £½ a million a year as a direct result of its affiliation to the centrist, federalist EPP (Christian Democrat) group. The internal finances of the parliament are so opaque that it has taken me two years to get to grips with the figures. Now that I have, they come as a bit of a shock.

Since 1992 British Tories have been associate members (under Rule 5b) of the EPP group, now renamed (in a purely cosmetic concession under the so-called Malaga agreement of July 1999) the EPP/ED. This means that we are free to vote a separate whip when we choose to do so, and in fact we do so around a third of the time. But parliamentary funding comes via the EPP group, who exercise a stranglehold on both finances and staffing.

It is argued that membership of the largest group in the parliament (232 members out of 626) gives us extra "clout" or "reach" or "throw weight" (choose your metaphor!). Or in the usual tired cliché, they say it enables us "to punch above our weight". But I and a number of colleagues believe that the opposite is true. On key committees in the parliament — the Conference of Presidents, spokesmen's meetings — we are represented by people who profoundly disagree with us. Our voice is unheard. Our light is hidden under a bushel.

The EPP recognises the British Conservatives as an anti-federalist virus in their body politic, and their immune system is working full time to isolate and marginalise us.

I have argued against membership of the EPP parliamentary group ever since I was elected as a Tory MEP in 1999.
We are told that being in a large group gives us access to key positions. It is probably true that in a smaller group we should not get the biggest plums — Caroline Jackson does a super job as Chairman of the important Environment Committee, for example (although our Co-Chairmanship of the ACP delegation is of less obvious political utility) — but the overall value of the posts we get is going to be much the same in a small group as in a large one, under the arcane *d'Hondt* system. Certainly smaller groups like the Greens seem to get their fair share of the prizes.

The EPP's control of our staffing is a running sore. New applicants are vetted by current staff, creating a self-sustaining bureaucrat caste. We are served by committed federalists whose personal agendas, no matter how professionally they dissimulate, are inimical to our own. And they are not always entirely professional. Recently, and disgracefully, a senior EPP *apparatchik* attached to the Tory delegation briefed the press against an independent Irish MEP from his own group, Rosemary (Dana) Scallon, after the federalist camp was infuriated by her successful support for the Irish NO campaign.

In one recent celebrated case Conservative MEPs were so incensed by the EPP's staffing run-around that virtually the whole Tory delegation voted to reject the EPP's preferred candidate for a new appointment — and one of the short-list offered to us by the EPP was actually a card-carrying member of the Lib-Dems! By contrast the British Lib-Dems in the European Parliament have complete control of their own staffing within the Liberal group.

But the issue of money is the clearest and most blatant handicap of all. The EPP group receives around 57k euros *per capita* per year from the parliament for its MEPs (both full and associate members). These funds cover the group's operations, including staff, admin costs, publications, conferences and "study days" (although the main costs of "study days" in exotic locations like Paris, Rome and Thessalonika are borne from the individual MEPs' travel budgets).

And the EPP passes on only 25k euros (44%) to the British delegation. It keeps 32k euros (£19k). Across 35 British members, that amounts to around £670,000 a year. The British delegation also gets a share of any EPP group under-spend at the end of the year.

The under-spend is currently an issue between the EPP and the Tory group, since it appears that in some years since 1992 a significant part of the under-spend has gone to the Schumann Group, an ultra-federalist clique within the EPP, thus reducing the *pro-rata* rebate to the British Tories.

However it is untrue (contrary to what we were told in 1999) that we get more funding as a result of being in the largest group. The exact reverse is true. Smaller groups actually get **more** *per capita* — not unreasonable, as they lack the economies of scale available to the largest groups. In fact the average non-EPP member attracts 6,220 euros **more** than an EPP member. It is reasonable to assume that if the Tories were to leave the EPP and form a new group, they would benefit by about this amount, which grosses up to over £130,000. This more than offsets the anticipated refund of EPP under-spend for 2001.

We are left with the conclusion that our membership of the EPP is costing us at least £670,000 a year. There are tight parliamentary regulations on how this money can be spent — it could not just be mailed to Central Office. But it is money that could be supporting the Conservative cause, but is in fact being spent by the EPP in support of the federalist cause.

Now it goes without saying that in a smaller group outside the EPP the Tory delegation would have to provide some of the central administrative services that it currently receives from the EPP — although it is quite difficult to see what these services are, and they are nothing like half a million pounds' worth. Certainly the EPP employs lots of staff, but Tory colleagues frequently comment on how little value we get from them. In particular, standards of analysis of current parliamentary business seem to be much better in smaller parliamentary groups than what we get from the EPP's much larger staff.

If we were to engage our own staff out of the additional money, we could be sure they were on-side and that they were working with us, not against us.

Two things are certain: if we were to form a new group outside the EPP, we should have substantial change out of our lost £670,000. And we could be sure that all the money to which we are entitled is spent promoting Conservative values and objectives, instead of seeing half of it siphoned off to promote European federalism and integration.

Conservative activists who work their fingers to the bone running coffee mornings that raise £150 will be astonished to learn that we are passing up this huge sum which we could have for the taking.

There are MEPs from many member states who share our Conservative vision of a Europe of independent nation states, trading and co-operating together. They are saddened and bewildered that we, the largest anti-integrationist *bloc*, continue to sit with the federalists. If we were to leave the EPP and run up our own flag, dozens would rally to us. A Conservative parliamentary group might have up to seventy members, making it the third group in the parliament.

With our own staff, our own funding, and a shared Conservative vision of Europe, such a group would have real clout, and be able to defend democracy, independence and self-determination. ❧❧❧

The following article appeared in the December 2001 issue of the European Journal

Conservatives and the EPP: Miles Apart

"Come out from among them, and be ye separate, saith the Lord" (2nd Corinthians 6,17)

There has been a great debate in the Conservative Party, and especially amongst Conservative Euro-MPs, about the relationship between the Tory MEP delegation and the centrist, federalist EPP parliamentary group. Debate has centred around the key question of political differences, plus issues around funding and staffing, where the EPP has a stranglehold on the Tory delegation.

Many observers feel that the debate has generated more heat than light, and much of what has passed for rational analysis has in fact been highly subjective. But preliminary results of a study of MEPs' voting records undertaken by Dr. Simon Hix at the London School of Economics suddenly throws an objective, dispassionate and academic light on a murky area.

Dr. Hix has used a statistical technique which has previously been used successfully to analyse voting behaviour over time in the US Congress.

The research may be impartial and academic, yet its conclusion could hardly be more dramatic. Most major political groups in the parliament are coherent amongst themselves, and clearly distinct from all other groups. Uniquely, the

EPP-ED group (including the Tories) is quite clearly split into two sub-groups, which not surprisingly consist respectively of the Tories, and the rest of the EPP. Not only that, but the Tories are at least as distant from the EPP as the EPP is from the Liberals.

This is perfectly illustrated on Dr. Hix's scatter chart, which unfortunately cannot be reproduced here for copyright reasons. It is however accessible on his website at www.lse.ac.uk/depts/eprg. Go to 'EPRG Research Projects' and click on 'How MEPs Vote' and then go to the link titled 'Colour Figures of the NOMINATE plots'. On a square grid, the east/west axis is simply left versus right. The north/south axis represents federalist (north) versus anti-federalist (south). For each MEP, Dr. Hix has analysed voting records over the current parliament (1999 – 2001), and placed a point on the chart.

Imagine the chart as a clock face. On the left, around nine o'clock, we see the Greens and the hard-left groups, somewhat overlapping. At eleven o'clock, the close-packed forces of the European Socialists. At twelve o'clock, the Liberal group. At one o'clock, the EPP, almost as close-packed and coherent as the socialists and liberals. And then, around three o'clock, the Tories – close to each other, but a country mile from the EPP. In the south-east we have a scattering of minor groups and independents.

A separate analysis of national political delegations confirms the separation between Tories and the EPP, and throws up some additional points. On this analysis, Jim Nicholson, the single Ulster Unionist MEP, is close to the Tories but leaning a little toward the EPP, while the Irish independent Rosemary (Dana) Scallon, a heroine of the Irish NO Campaign, stands like a solitary but indomitable atoll in the clear blue water between the Tories and the EPP.

An interesting sidelight of this analysis: the British Lib-Dem delegation stands at the top left-hand corner of other European Liberal delegations: they are the most leftist and most federalist delegation in the ELDR.

In one sense the scatter-chart actually **under**estimates the difference between the Tories and the EPP. Under the terms of our "associate membership" of the EPP, we are entitled to have a separate Tory whip, and frequently do. But the EPP whip is always the starting point and the default position. Inevitably, therefore, the EPP voting line gets the benefit of any doubt. There can be little question that if the Tory delegation approached each vote with a clean sheet of paper, instead of with an EPP whip, we should vote differently from the EPP even more often – and our splodge on the scatter-chart would move further south-east.

The debate on the relationship between the Tories and the EPP will rumble on, but it is now informed by fact as well as opinion. To all intents and purposes, based on their voting record, the Tories do in fact form a separate group in the parliament. Politically, they are as distinct from the EPP as the EPP from the Liberals, and more distinct from the EPP than the liberals from the socialists, for example.

This raises another potential problem for the troubled Tory/EPP relationship. The European Court of Justice recently ruled that the so-called "Technical Group of Independents" (TGI) did not qualify as a *bona fide* group in the European parliament, since it was based not on political affinity but on administrative convenience. Members of the TGI had formed their group not to pursue common aims but merely to exploit parliamentary rules, which favour groups rather than individuals.

Based on this precedent, Dr. Hix's research creates a *prima facie* case that the Tory/EPP link is also merely a technical link to exploit the rules, rather than a genuine coalition based on common political objectives. It may well be open to challenge by the parliamentary authorities, or indeed by other political groups in the parliament.

But the key conclusion is inescapable. Regardless of the arguments over staff and funding, and based not on subjective opinions, but on a hard-edged academic analysis of actual voting patterns, **the Tories are already in effect a separate political group,** quite distinct from the EPP. It is time for this undeniable fact to be reflected within the parliament's organisation. ✌✌

This research programme is being run by Dr. Simon Hix, Department of Government, London School of Economics and Political Science,
Houghton Street,
London
WC2A 2AE

Tel: *0207 955 7657*
Fax: *0207 831 1701*

It is carried out under the auspices of the European Parliament Research Group, a twenty-plus member transatlantic and pan-European research team. A full report is expected early in 2002.

In May 2001, the parliament dealt with the Schleicher report on pan-European political parties — a typical federalist measure to build the Euro-super-state. This article appeared in the European Journal of April 2001

European Political Parties
A major building-block of the Super-state

There have been proposals around for the formation of pan-European political parties from at least as early as 1996, when the Tsatsos report was prepared by the European parliament's Committee on Institutional Affairs. It is important at the outset to distinguish between political **parties**, and political **groups** in the European parliament (EP). Most national political parties represented within the EP form part of a parliamentary group. For example Labour sit with the PSE (Party of European socialists), while Tories are associate (but not full) members of the EPP/ED group.

European political parties, on the other hand, exist outside the parliament. Clearly where both a group in the EP and a corresponding political party exist, there will be close links between them, as there are in the UK between Westminster parties and national parties, but they are plainly not the same thing. There is already European funding in place both for MEPs and for political groups in the EP. The proposals now on the table, in the Schleicher report currently before the EP, are for European political parties, not for groups in the EP.

The definition of a European party is clearly set out. Such a party must have representation in the European parliament, or in national or regional parliaments, in at least five member states, or have achieved at least 5% of the vote in at least five member states at the last European elections. The British Conservative Party clearly does not qualify.

One of the justifications advanced for these new funding proposals (currently 7 million Euros) is that money intended for groups in the EP actually leaks out into external parties, and that these new proposals will make for transparency. It is not made clear how spending additional money will necessarily ensure that the existing money is spent more transparently. It is rather as if one proposed to fix a leaky boat by pouring more water into the hull.

According to Schleicher's report, these Euro-parties are to be "an outlet for European public opinion". Clearly Mrs Schleicher was not familiar with John Stuart Mill, who remarked in the 19th century that *"where peoples lack fellow feeling, and especially where they speak and read different languages, the common public opinion necessary for representative government cannot exist"*. Enoch Powell in the 20th century and Roger Scruton in the 21st have echoed similar sentiments. They are clearly right, which is why the very idea of "European democracy" is a non-starter, and why European political parties are unnecessary (although of course loose federations of like-minded national parties, as for example the IDU, have a rôle to play).

41

Clearly the whole motivation behind the project is to add a new building-block to the edifice of federalism, to the European super-state. We have, or are getting, a European flag, passport and anthem. We have common agricultural, social and employment policies, a common foreign and security policy, a European legal system, a common currency and a central bank, and a European Army. Gerhardt Schroder has called for a European Constitution and a European government. What more natural in this brave new world than the call for European political parties?

A proposed amendment to the Schleicher report required assent to the so-called Charter of Fundamental Rights as a criterion for funding — ruling out the Tory party at a stroke. There are provisions for a committee of "wise men", or perhaps the EP itself, to judge whether a particular party qualifies or not. Many Euro-realists fear that this is a ploy to exclude them, and to pay European tax-payers' money directly to integrationist parties.

The report contains some superficial reassurance on this point. It says: *"Parties need not necessarily be advocates of European integration; Euro-sceptical parties may also be supported if their policies focus on issues of European integration"*. The reassurance is short-lived, however. On an earlier page we read: *"They (Euro-parties) are seen as instrumental in securing public support for the European integration project"*. So that's all right then. And remember it will be either federalist "wise men" or the federalist EP which will decide on eligibility.

There is a more fundamental reason why this whole proposal is a gross, biased and anti-democratic attempt to direct funds to parties supporting integration and away from Euro-critical parties. Federalist parties want pan-European institutions, and see Euro-parties as a natural part of the structure of the future European polity. For equally obvious reasons, Euro-critical parties see the focus of democratic accountability as the nation-state, and are therefore deeply reluctant to form trans-national parties. For the Euro-realist, the very idea of a trans-national party (as distinct from an association of national parties) is a contradiction of democracy.

Thus, *de facto* if not *de jure*, virtually all of this new funding will go directly to promote integration. And it may even tend to force reluctant national parties into uncomfortable international liaisons.

Clearly, therefore, the proposal is inimical to the Conservative party, and any Tory worth his salt could be expected to fight it tooth and nail. Curious, therefore, to note that one or two voices in the Party fought hard to have the MEP group abstain on Schleicher. Their reasoning was that if we voted against, it might prejudice our right to future funding (even though we are not part of any trans-national party and are thus disqualified to start with).

This argument is patently spurious. On this reasoning a Westminster MP who voted against an increase in MPs' salaries would not be entitled to claim the increase, and if he voted against Blair's Baby Bond, his children would be denied that privilege. The fact is that the law is the same for all, whether we voted against it or not.

It is astonishing that there are still those who deny that a super-state is the final destination of the federalist project, despite the fact that virtually every attribute of the nation state either exists, or is being created, at the European level. European political parties should therefore come as no surprise.

The Schleicher report was the subject of an extraordinary procedural ambush in the Strasbourg plenary on May 16th (2001), planned and executed by a group of committed Euro-realist Tory MEPs plus like-minded colleagues from other member-states and parties.

Around 4:30 p.m., when the Schleicher debate was scheduled to start, there were, as usual, very few members in the chamber. Debates in Strasbourg are typically attended only by those with speaking time, intent on reading their statement into the record. (The others are not lying in the sun — they are caught up in the lunatic maelstrom of meetings that characterises the EP). Some thirty or so Euro-realist MEPs entered the chamber, and one, a Portuguese, Ribiero e Castro, proposed a motion that the report should be "referred back" to Committee.

The leader of the European Socialist group Baron Crespo (counter-intuitively, not a patent snack food), seeking to head off the resolution, called the quorum, as he was entitled to do. There were clearly too few MEPs present to form a quorum. However under the EP's arcane rules, a valid quorum call must be supported by at least 32 members, who indicate their support by standing up. (Don't even ask what happens if fewer than 32 are in the Chamber to start with!).

Only about a dozen stood, with the plotters sitting on their hands, so the quorum call failed, the vote proceeded, and despite frantic efforts by the acting chairman Mr. Vidal Quadras, of the EPP/ED group, to find a procedural let-out, we won the vote. At a group meeting the next day, Vidal Quadras admitted that he had delayed as long as was decent in the hope that the federalist cavalry would arrive, but in the end had no option but to allow the vote — a fine piece of neutral chairmanship!

Our triumph was short-lived. The next day the powers-that-be used a disputed interpretation of Rule 111 to reinstate the report, and the debate took place around 10:30 a.m. In the voting at noon, the measure was passed by 352 to 82 with 18 abstentions (Tories voted against), and the amendment on the so-called Charter of Fundamental Rights was also passed on a show of hands, so that to qualify for funding, parties have to subscribe to an essentially socialist and corporatist document.

But May 17th was a great day nonetheless. We gave the federalists a bloody nose, and showed them that de Gaulle's dream of a *Europe des patries* is not yet dead. ༚༝༚༝༚༝

The European Union has a rotating presidency under which each member state gets a six-month turn to steer the ship. In order to provide continuity it operates a "troika" including the preceding and following presidencies.

Each new presidency comes in with high ambitions, usually not realised. Tony Blair's British presidency in Jan/June 1998 was particularly disappointing. But in a conspicuous triumph of hope over experience, incoming presidencies love to set out grandiose ambitions at the beginning of their half-year in the limelight.

At the beginning of the Portuguese presidency (Jan/June 2000), and again at the beginning of the Belgian presidency (July/December 2001) I felt moved to warn readers about what they should expect.

Here Come the Portuguese!

The rotating presidency of the EU rolls round to Portugal for the first six months of 2000. To introduce their plans they have issued a densely packed 29-page document in fractured English (you'll be interested to know that they're concerned about "democraticity", for example). One of the joys of the MEP's life is the opportunity to study such documents.

Most of it is motherhood-and-apple-pie stuff, generalised positive aims that no one much could take issue with. But lurking in the endless paragraphs are warning signs – often couched in terms that may only be clear to insiders.

I would hate East Midlands electors to miss these gems, so here are some of them.

- **Preservation of the European social model.** This is the same social model that has delivered stubbornly high unemployment on the continent, at double the UK level. The same social model that ties the hands of industry, small business and agriculture with a mass of regulation and red tape. The social model that threatens European competitiveness in

44

the global economy. The social model that contrasts so badly with our own "Anglo-Saxon" approach. But they're determined to keep it.

- **Promoting a sense of European citizenship.** In other words, propaganda paid for out of your taxes to convince you and me what a fine thing Europe is and what huge benefits it delivers to all of us. You may well feel that we should be left to judge for ourselves.

- **A European dimension in education.** Similar to the above, but now they're going to get at our children in school with their propaganda. This is in direct contravention of the 1944 Education Act, which requires a balanced approach on controversial issues. But don't worry. In the event of any challenge, the European Court will rule in favour of the European project.

- **The rôle of culture in the European project…development of a European cultural identity**. Again, similar to the above – forcing propaganda down our throats. But they also want to erect protectionist barriers around our entertainment industries, restrict the percentage of foreign (for which read American) content, and tell us what we can watch on television. You may feel that it is more important to defend choice and diversity, and to protect the rich patchwork of national cultures within Europe, than to develop a European cultural identity.

- **Extension of qualified majority voting.** This means scrapping the British veto, so that the majority view is imposed on us whether we like it or not.

- **Co-ordination of macro-economic, structural and employment policies.** This means having unelected and unaccountable bureaucrats in Brussels deciding Britain's economic policies, instead of our elected representatives.

- **Proper functioning of the Single Market…in the tax field. Obtaining concrete results for the tax package as soon as possible.** This means imposing damaging new taxes on the UK, and eventually having all our taxes set by Brussels (see above).

It goes on. A common asylum policy. A common crime prevention policy. Strengthening the role of Europol (the nascent European federal police force). The development of "minimal social rules". A European policy of Security and Defence … with a credible operational capacity (i.e. a European Army).

Don't say we didn't warn you. It's all there in black and white. ❧❧❧

Watch Out — Here Come the Belgians!

I still meet people in the East Midlands who say "Europe is a long way away — it doesn't matter to me". They are amazed to learn that more than half of the new legislation that affects us in the East Midlands comes from Brussels, not Westminster. Last year around 4000 statutory instruments implementing Brussels laws were nodded through in Westminster. That's about twenty each working day, so you can guess how little effective scrutiny they get.

In Brussels, the powers-that-be are crying into their beer over the Irish referendum result and the consequent delays to further integration. They know there's a problem with public opinion, but they have the quaint idea that people would learn to love the EU if only they understood it better. My experience is that the more the public learn about the EU, the more alarmed they get. And I regard it as a key part of my job to make sure they know as much as possible.

With this in mind, I have been looking at the plans of the new Belgian presidency of the EU. (The presidency rotates every six months — the Swedes are just bowing out and the ultra-federalist Belgians taking over). I have looked carefully at a speech made by Belgian Prime Minister Guy Verhofstadt, and at a memorandum produced by the three Benelux countries (including Belgium), both in June this year.

There are some real gems. "We would like to see the European project rooted in a constitution" says the memo. Mr. Verhofstadt goes further: "I do not understand those who oppose a European constitution. Each country has one...the EU must have one too". Leaving aside the fact that Britain has no written constitution, Mr. V. seems to have missed the key point — it is precisely *because* a constitution defines a nation that we can't allow the EU to have one. An EU constitution would be the foundation of the super-state.

And for good measure Mr. V. adds "Let there be no doubt about it. I am greatly in favour of further European integration". He adds that he supports subsidiarity — leaving defined powers with the member-states. He even tells us which policies should be left to national governments: sport, culture, education. So that's all right then. Westminster can do tennis and tiddly-winks, while Brussels does tax and trade.

"The treaty of Nice has to be ratified" says the memo. Never mind that the Irish have voted it down, and that under the terms of the existing EU treaties the new treaty therefore falls. Just like the Danes in 1992, when they voted against Maastricht, the hapless Irish will be told to vote again until they get the right answer. The contempt shown by the EU institutions for the opinions and aspirations of ordinary people, for the democratic rights of voters, is positively breathtaking.

As my South East Region colleague Dan Hannan MEP puts it, the objective of EU enlargement is to extend democracy and the rule of law to the central and eastern European accession countries. And yet the EU is perfectly happy to dump democracy and the rule of law in order to get on with it.

Mr. V. recognises that "There is a gap between the European Union and its citizens", but goes on to say "Ideas which a few years ago were taboo and rejected outright as fantasies of Euro-fanatics, like an EU constitution, an EU asylum policy or an EU Public Prosecutor, are now being advocated without restraint....Clearly, the minds are going in the right direction".

The minds of the bureaucrats may be going Mr. V's way, but not the minds of voters I meet in the East Midlands. The EU's leaders are calling for a wide-ranging debate, but like the Irish referendum they're prepared to accept only one answer — more integration, more centralisation, more harmonisation. And an end to our right to have a say in our own affairs. Democracy and self-determination are under threat in the 21st-century EU as never before. ❧❧❧

"Integration is inevitable...it is impossible to stop the trend".

Now who could that be? Jacques Delors in 1995? Helmut Kohl in 1998? Joshka Fischer in 2000? Romano Prodi in 2001? No, actually. It was von Ribbentrop in 1941!

Chapter Five

Tory Policy on the EU

I have returned time and again to a basic proposition. It is not enough simply to put a stop to European integration. It has gone much too far. The Conservative party must commit itself, clearly and unambiguously, to a policy of radical renegotiation. The following article appeared in June 2000.

Reversing the Ratchet of Integration

The European Parliament's report on the current Intergovernmental Conference (IGC) was described by the Daily Telegraph as "the most federalist document ever to come out of an EU institution". I voted against it, as did the great majority of Tory MEPs.

The IGC will lead in December to the Treaty of Nice. We can't yet be sure what will be in it, but the Parliament's report gives us an idea. It will probably include the end of the national veto in all except treaty changes; tax harmonisation; strengthened common foreign policy and "defence identity" (= European army); a European Public Prosecutor and strengthened Europol to pursue "crimes against the EU" (sinister thought!); regulation and funding of Europe-wide political parties with sanctions against those judged not to be sufficiently committed to "European values".

These sanctions could easily be applied against the Tory party. There are echoes here of the old Eastern block. They didn't ban elections. They just banned parties that opposed the government.

Along with the Treaty comes the so-called Charter of Fundamental Rights – as if we didn't have enough rights with the UN Declaration and the EU Convention. But this will be about "economic and social rights" – it will enshrine socialism in European law. It will roll back the reforms of the Thatcher years. It will further undermine UK courts. It will give the notoriously interventionist European Court of Justice a foundation on which it can build a vast superstructure of interpretation and precedent. In other words, it will pass responsibility for law making from elected representatives to unelected and federalist judges. Worst of all, it will amount virtually to a Constitution for a European State.

The Tory party is wholly opposed to the Charter, and even Labour is against writing it into the Treaty, but most of our partners want it in. Again, most Tory MEPs and I voted against the Charter.

The Treaty and the Charter are bad news, but we have good news too. William Hague has said that the next Conservative government will not transfer further powers to Brussels without a referendum. Francis Maude says that unless the British people approve the Nice Treaty, we will feel free to unpick it. And defence spokesman Iain Duncan Smith says we will pull out of the European Army.

The Party has crossed an important threshold here. Not only will we halt **future** integration – we will roll back **existing** measures in key areas. Like it or not, that means renegotiation.

Those who argue that renegotiation is impossible are being naïve and defeatist. The whole European project involves continuous renegotiation. Unfortunately, it's mainly in the wrong direction. But not always. They said that Margaret Thatcher couldn't negotiate a rebate -- but she did. John Major got opt-outs on the Social Chapter, Schengen and the Euro.

Renegotiation is not code for withdrawal. But the threat of withdrawal may be necessary to achieve it. If we can convince our partners that we will have membership on our terms or not at all, they will fall over themselves to accommodate us.

It is clear that membership on current terms is bad for Britain, even allowing for the admitted benefits of free trade in the Single Market. The Institute of Directors estimates the current net cost of membership as between £15 and £25 billion a year. The status quo – the mad dash to a federal super-state – is clearly unacceptable to the British people. Renegotiation is vital, for unless we achieve a looser and more flexible relationship within the EU – like the Common Market we voted for in 1975 – then calls for withdrawal may indeed become irresistible. ॐॐॐ

I had covered the same theme earlier, in April 2000

Why We Must Renegotiate

There seems to be a gap at the heart of Tory policy on Europe, and it needs to be addressed before we firm up the manifesto for the next General Election.

In his famous speech in Budapest in 1999, William Hague appeared to be saying that the essence of EU membership was the acceptance of the "rights and responsibilities of the Single Market", and that all other areas of EU policy should be available to member-states on a menu-driven, pick'n'mix basis. He argued, rightly, that much of the rest of the *acquis communautaire* would stand in the way of enlargement. Clearly it will be impossible to extend the CAP in its current form to Poland, with its huge capacity for agricultural production. Nor is it credible to extend European social policy, damaging as it is even to advanced western economies, to the developing economies of the East.

However, recent formulations of policy say that the next Conservative government will seek a flexibility clause which will allow us to opt-out of *NEW* integrationist initiatives. This is a huge retreat from "only the rights and responsibilities of the Single Market". It would mean:

That we accept the whole of the existing *acquis communautaire* as it stands today – the social chapter, the common foreign and security policy and so on

That we give a blank cheque for any new integrationist measures that may come up between now and the next Tory government – and while I am hopeful that we can win the next general election, we must recognise that this *could* mean 2005, by which time Britain may no longer exist as an independent sovereign nation. In particular, we should be accepting the outcome of the Treaty of Nice (December 2000).

Clearly an embargo on *new* integrationist measures after 2005 would be shutting the stable door after national sovereignty had bolted.

I do not think that many Conservative Party members and activists, or indeed the British people, are inclined to accept the whole of the current *acquis*, and they would certainly not countenance the horrors of the proposed Treaty of Nice. The Nice proposals include pan-European parties and pan-European lists for European parliament elections, powers for the EU to take sanctions against elected governments of member-states (which could allow sanctions against a future Conservative government), a European prosecutor, and a wholesale surrender of national vetoes.

We urgently need to get the Party back to the "Single Market only" position. This is essential if we are to deliver our vision of a Europe of nation states. I also believe that it is essential if we want to set out a credible and attractive European policy for the next general election. I have lost count of the East Midlands electors, both within the party and outside it, who have said to me "We voted in the referendum for a Common Market, a free trade area, not for political union".

This means that the word **renegotiation** must have pride of place in our general election manifesto. We have been curiously coy about it in recent months. All Conservative MPs (except Edward Heath) voted against ratification of the Amster-dam Treaty in 1998. We were against it then – surely we are against it now, and surely therefore the next Conservative government must re-open it.

We should present our policies in a positive light, not as a rejection of Europe, but as a positive assertion of the powers and competences that we claim for the nation state. In my view, these must include social, employment, and industrial policy, economic and monetary policy, taxation, home affairs (no *corpus juris* or European prosecutor), asylum and immigration, foreign and security policy, defence, agriculture and fisheries. (We have said that we will "revisit" fisheries, but we seem reluctant to say plainly that we will repatriate fisheries policy and take back our territorial waters).

I think that we should also seek treaty changes that would convert the EU from a customs union into a free trade area, thus allowing us to negotiate a free trade deal with NAFTA. The ultimate objective should be a European Union that looks, at least from a British perspective, like a free trade area and nothing more.

Our opponents will of course say that this cannot be negotiated. Here I am afraid I go somewhat beyond party policy. I believe that if a future Conservative government is unable to negotiate a new settlement with Europe satisfactory to the British people, then, whether we like it or not, the question of continued British membership will arise. Our partners must understand that, and it will clarify their minds wonderfully on the issue. Personally I find it astonishing that some Conservatives appear to be unable to say "Never" to the Euro, and yet seem quite willing to say "Never" to withdrawal.

No sensible politician says Never. No policy is set in stone. All policies must be reviewed from time to time with an open mind, to see if they continue to serve the nation's interests.

A couple of words of caution. We need to be careful with the term "Single Market". As we use it in the UK or in the Tory party, we think of it as broadly synonymous with free trade. Of course viewed from the continental viewpoint, the Single Market is an almost infinitely elastic term. It can certainly be made to include industrial, social and employment policy, taxation, economic and monetary union, and so on. We need to be clear when we use the term in debate, especially with our partners, that we mean it in its minimalist British sense, and not in the inclusive continental sense. The rights and responsibilities we accept are those of a free trade area (or at worst a customs union) – not the centralisation and harmonisation of everything.

We must also be wary of "flexibility". In the UK it means opt-outs. In Brussels it means "enhanced co-operation", or fast-track integration.

If we believe in national sovereignty and a Europe of nations, then we have a duty to our people and to our nation to declare, boldly, clearly, proudly, that a Conservative government will radically renegotiate the treaties. This may also win us the election. ❧❧❧

I have always been frustrated by our tendency to wrap up European policy in cautious and non-contentious language. If we have a clear and attractive proposition, let's not blunt its edge with mealy-mouthed phrases. I love to use the phrase "European deconstruction", much to the embarrassment of some less robust colleagues.

Time for European Deconstruction

For some time now the Tory party has made it clear that Britain is close to the limits of European integration. We have said that the next Conservative government will demand a new flexibility clause in the EU treaties which would allow the UK to opt-out of new integrationist moves.

However many of us have felt that this does not go far enough, for two reasons. First of all, there is a huge amount in the existing treaties which works against the
British national interest. An obvious example would be the whole raft of EU social regulation, which at first sight appears to offer benefits to employees, but actually reduces competitiveness, productivity, prosperity and employment. It will make us all poorer in the end – witness the persistently high unemployment on the continent.

Secondly, the idea of an opt-out only on NEW legislation means we are giving a blank cheque to this Labour government to hand over new powers to the EU between now and the return of a Tory government. That could mean the up-coming Treaty of Nice, expected in December 2000, and the so-called Charter of Fundamental Rights that goes with it, which amounts almost to a constitution for a United States of Europe.

I have been arguing within the Party for some time that we had to go the extra mile, and not only commit to stopping new integration, but to be prepared to unwind it in existing areas. It seems the idea is catching on.

William Hague, in his speech to Welsh Tories on 9 June 2000, promised that any significant constitutional change in future would be put to the British people in a referendum. I have huge faith in British common sense, and I don't believe that the British people would vote to hand over new powers to Brussels, so this one initiative would stop the rot. But Francis Maude in his speech at the Humboldt university in Berlin on 8 June 2000 went further. He called for major changes in the CAP, national control over fisheries, and national control over foreign aid unless the EU can put its house in order. Most important, he said that unless the new Treaty of Nice is specifically approved by the British people, either in a referendum or a general election, then a Tory government will feel free to unpick it.

In a wonderful week for British sovereignty, we also had a robust speech from Tory defence spokesman Iain Duncan-Smith. He made it clear that while we support defence co-operation in Europe, we think that a common European Army, to which Labour has signed up, is merely a political stunt aimed at integration, and has no proper defence purpose. Indeed we believe that a new European defence capability and command structure would undermine NATO. We would therefore withdraw the UK from it.

So that is the conclusion. A future Conservative government will withdraw British armed forces from the tentacles of Brussels. It will insist on a referendum before any new powers can be handed over to the EU. And in key sectors it will start to roll back the treaties and take back national control over vital areas of policy. I am delighted. It was for these objectives that I gave up my business career and got into politics.

The great task of our generation is European deconstruction. The Conservative Party has started to address it. ❧❧❧

In the summer of 2001, Chris Heaton-Harris and I committed ourselves wholeheartedly to Iain Duncan Smith's leadership campaign. The successful outcome was a great satisfaction — and a great relief.

The Tory Party Finds Its Soul

I and my colleague Chris Heaton-Harris MEP spent the summer working our socks off in the East Midlands to support Iain Duncan Smith in the Conservative leadership election. We mailed party members, spoke to meetings, gave media interviews. When the news came through on Wednesday that Iain had won by 61% to 39%, we were relieved and delighted. We had become increasingly confident in the last few weeks of the campaign that Iain was ahead, but nagging doubts remained until the declaration.

Don't assume that the 39% of Tories who voted for Ken Clarke supported his extremist European policies. I know a lot of Eurosceptic party members who voted for Ken, holding their noses on his European policy, but believing that he was warm and cuddly enough to win a general election. I respect their view, but I think they're wrong.

The fact is that Iain stands right in the centre of Conservative opinion on Europe, and that means that he reflects the views of about 70% of the UK population. We want trade and co-operation with Europe, but we don't want to be governed from Brussels, we don't want a Euro-Army and we don't want to scrap the Pound.

Because Iain stands four-square on this common ground, he can now draw a line under the debate that has bedevilled us for ten years. Yes, there will still be a few old dinosaurs who disagree, but the Tories are actually more united than Labour on Europe, and far more so than the Lib-Dems — opinion polls show that most Lib-Dem voters actually disagree with the party's extreme federalist position.

That means that Iain can close the book on Euro-squabbles, and actually start to talk about the issues that matter to voters on the doorstep — schools, hospitals, crime, transport, the environment. And already during the leadership campaign he's been setting out exciting and radical ideas that will revitalise our policy agenda.

Iain may be a Eurosceptic, but he's perfectly happy to look at how our European partners deliver education and health-care, and to learn lessons from them. And in fact they do a lot better than us. How? They have a mixed system of state and private provision, in some cases based on insurance schemes, and always respecting the right to education and healthcare free at the point of delivery for all who want it.

On health, for example, Britain spends as much as most continental governments — but they bring in additional money from the private sector, and deliver hugely superior choice, quality and service. The truth is that state monopolies don't work any better in health and education than they worked in airlines and telephones. Yet this current Labour government, that constantly bangs on about modernisation, is wedded to a fifty-year-old system of health provision which looks positively antiquated compared to our European partners.

Iain has set out exciting new proposals on the environment — and won plaudits from Friends of the Earth. Contrasting with Labour's top-down approach, and their damaging new energy taxes, Iain wants to harness the goodwill of ordinary people in a bottom-up approach. For example, why not offer tax-breaks for solar power installations on domestic and commercial roof-space, and turn Britain's roofs into a clean, renewable power station?

This is the kind of new thinking which will reach out beyond the Tory core vote, to young and uncommitted voters for whom the environment matters.

Of course now that Iain has won, we must be prepared for the Labour onslaught. Sadly, much of the script they'll use has already been written by Ken Clarke, in the attacks he made on Iain during the contest. They'll say he's right-wing and anti-Europe. But the public won't be taken in. Iain is not right-wing — he's reasonable and pragmatic, with a good dose of common sense. Nor is he anti-Europe. But he wants a Europe that works for ordinary people, not for distant and unaccountable foreign bureaucrats and institutions.

Now is the time for all Conservatives, and indeed for everyone who believes in their country's independence and self-determination, everyone who believes we should keep our own currency, to rally behind the new Conservative leader and ensure that we replace this failing Labour government at the next general election. ॐ॰ॐ॰ॐ

According to Stephen Roberts, Professor of
Modern History at the University of Sydney, in his book
The House That Hitler Built,
"Hitler developed the idea of establishing regions of Europe
as a means of destroying national identities".
As the French say,
plus ça change, plus c'est la même chose!

Chapter Six

Labour Policy on the EU

Colleagues in the party sometimes debate which is the greatest enemy — socialism or feder-alism? In a sense it is a pointless debate. Both socialism and federalism are hugely inimical to the interests of the British people. But unless we reassert our national inde-pendence, we may find we're no longer in a position to oppose socialism at home. This chapter, I hope, attacks the Labour party, and federalism, in equal measure.

The following two pieces were written in the heady days when Keith Vaz, a Leicester MP, was Labour's Minister for Europe.

Keith Vaz's 3½ Million Phantom Jobs

Keith Vaz, described as Minister for Europe, says that if Britain were to leave the European Union, three and a half million jobs would go. This wild scare story doesn't bear a moment's examination. I've been wondering which jobs actually depend on our membership of the EU. Well obviously, Keith Vaz's job. That's one. Then there are 87 MEPs. Their jobs would go. Maybe a couple of hundred assistants attached to the MEPs. And a few hundred jobs of various officials in government, a few European Officers with local coun-cils, a few dozen in Euro Information Centres.

If you make really generous estimates, maybe three and a half thousand all up. But three and a half *million*? Come on, Keith, wake up and smell the coffee!

What Mr. Vaz means, of course, is that there may be 3½ million jobs in companies that export to Europe. But of course there are also millions of jobs in America, and in China, and in Japan that depend on exports to the EU. Keith Vaz's wild claim assumes that if we were to leave the EU, we'd stop trading with it. But that's a daft assumption. You don't have to accept integration and loss of sovereignty in an anti-democratic European state in order to trade with Europe. And we buy far more from Europe than Europe buys from us, so there could be no question of any petulant anti-UK reaction from our EU partners.

The truth is that exports from the USA to continental Europe have grown faster in recent years than exports from the UK. You don't have to be a member to do business with the EU, and countries that are not members may actually do better than countries that are.

So should we leave the EU? Not at least until we have had a thorough go at reforming it. President Romano Prodi, ably supported by Tony Blair, is on a pilgrimage to his Holy Belgian Empire. We in the Conservative Party have an alternative vision of a flexible Europe of nation states, where co-operation rather than centralisation is the watch-word. We want an outward-looking, competitive Europe. We want an end to excessive regulation. We want flexible labour markets which generate jobs and prosperity.

The next Conservative government will argue vigorously for that vision of Europe. But it will be up to the British people to judge whether, in the end, we succeed. If they judge that the European Union is beyond reform, then the question of our future membership will inevitably arise. ❧❧

Vaz All at Sea in Euro-debate

For months I'd been trying to nail down a debate with Keith Vaz MP, Labour's Minister for Europe, who as MP for Leicester East is also one of my East Midlands constituents. I wanted to ask him why Labour says it sees no constitutional barrier to Britain joining the Euro – but it won't say why not!

I was delighted therefore when he agreed to a public debate on Friday March 2nd 2001 at Leicester University, chaired by the Deputy Editor of the Leicester Mercury, Jeremy Clifford. I spoke first, setting out the profound economic and constitutional barriers to Britain joining the Euro, and I was disappointed when Mr. Vaz, in his speech, talked around the issues without really answering the question. We all know, of course, that Labour is determined to run a general election campaign without mentioning the Euro!

But the real shocker came during questions from the public (and although a number of my supporters were there, I promise I didn't plant any of the questions!). Mr. Vaz, Labour's Minister for Europe, showed an amazing ignorance of his own party's policies on European issues.

Someone asked if Mr. Vaz would set out Gordon Brown's famous five economic tests for entering the Euro. He managed three of them, and started to flounder. I helped out with a fourth (protecting the City of London and UK financial markets), but the fifth remained elusive. Asked what objective criteria would be applied to judge if the tests were met, Mr. Vaz said he was a politician not an economist, so couldn't answer!

Another questioner asked about funding for the proposed Euro referendum, and it was immediately clear that Mr. Vaz simply did not know that his own government has set down rules for referendum spending, or that those rules are unfairly skewed to favour a YES vote. He said that obviously funding should be equal for both sides, and ventured the personal view that the government should fund it. I hope Gordon Brown never finds out what Mr. Vaz said – he'd be furious!

Asked about the famous EU Rickety Ladders Directive, Mr. Vaz dismissed it as a Euro-myth like straight bananas or square tomatoes. I had to explain to Mr. Vaz that I myself had sat on the European Parliament's Employment Committee when the measure was passed (I voted against!), and that the *rapporteur* on the Directive was actually a British Labour MEP, Peter Skinner. And I have now sent Mr. Vaz a copy of the EU's straight bananas directive!

Mr. Vaz got very upset when I described the EU's so-called Charter of Fundamental Rights, pointing out Article 52, which gives the EU the power to suspend our rights without challenge or due process, and I dared to mention that the constitution for Nazi Germany had a very similar clause. He said this comparison was offensive and repugnant, and called on me to retract (and has since been briefing the press about my "distasteful references to Hitler").

I declined to retract, on the grounds that what I had said was both true and important. Mr. Vaz should think about the message before he shoots the messenger. Why is Labour supporting this profoundly illiberal Charter which threatens our democratic freedoms? Mr. Vaz once said that the Charter "Had no more legal force than the Beano", yet the European Courts are already taking it into account.

However, for good measure I was able to offer Mr. Vaz a parallel between the Nazis and New Labour. The last person in Europe to ban fox-hunting was – guess who – Adolf Hitler! ❧❧❧

Labour's Regional Plot

"If the answer's more politicians, we're asking the wrong question", as John Major famously said. Yet that's exactly what Labour is planning for Britain. Already we have eleven Regional Development Agencies (RDAs), each with very similar, formulaic, politically-correct "Strategies", each producing glossy booklets outlining its achievements.

And with each RDA, we have a "Regional Assembly" where local worthies get together, supposedly to monitor the performance of the RDA, but in fact to relish a sense of their own importance, and to enjoy coffee and biscuits. As it happens, I get to sit on the East Midlands Assembly, because I am an MEP, and I've been to a couple of their meetings.

They didn't seem to do a great deal of monitoring. In fact it seemed halfway between a Saga tour and a Sunday School: "Off you go, children, into your groups, look at the question you've been given and come back with your answers". So off we went into our groups and tried to work out which were the best cultural attractions of the East Midlands. At the feedback session someone suggested fox-hunting, which was greeted with a sharp intake of breath.

All the emphasis seems to be internalised: liaising and co-operating and conferencing and sharing best practice. The moment you have two committees you have to have a Liaison Officer to co-ordinate between them. They spend their time taking in each other's washing, with very little about outcomes, about actual results that matter to ordinary people.

Regions are curious entities. Too big to worry about refuse collection, but too small to handle inward investment effectively. They lack any resonance with ordinary people. I find that voters in Louth, for example, have a strong sense of identity with Lincolnshire. But they don't feel any particular affinity with Glossop or Hinckley, at opposite ends of the East Midlands. We can understand a County Council, and feel that in some way it represents our interests. But the East Midlands? Where's that?

But now the Labour government is hell-bent on replacing these appointed Assemblies with *elected* Assemblies. More politicians, more bureaucrats, more expense vouchers, more spending. Did anybody ask you if you wanted your taxes spent on an elected Regional Assembly? No. I thought not. And as soon as they've got these Assemblies up and running, they'll realise there's too much local government, and they'll scrap the County Councils.

Typical Labour modernisation. Take something comfortable and familiar, with an established track record, and scrap it, and replace it with something untried and unwanted.

So who wants Regional Assemblies? Well of course all the people who smell jobs and power and status and money. But also, of course, the European Union.

When I went to Brussels as a candidate before the 1999 Euro-election, a Tory MEP said to me "Roger, in ten years time there will be no Westminster parliament. We'll have a Britain of regions governed from Brussels". That's why

Brussels is so keen to cement links with RDAs and Regional Assemblies, inviting members to visit, and buttering them up. That's why the regions are opening expensive liaison offices in Brussels.

It's all part of the master-plan to by-pass Westminster, to eviscerate the nation-state, and to create the vision of a Europe of regions governed from Brussels, where the nation-state is no more than a quaint anachronism.

We should oppose Labour's regional agenda because there is no public appetite for it, because it is costly and wasteful, but above all because it is designed to undermine the nation-state, and with it our independence and democracy. ❧❧❧

A Liberal View

At a press briefing in Nottingham in October 2001, organised by the London office of the European parliament (yes, I'm afraid there is a London office of the European parliament!), conversation over lunch turned to Labour's regional plans. Naturally, the Labour MEPs backed it to the hilt. I opposed it.

Turncoat MEP Bill Newton Dunn, now a Liberal, sought a middle way. He liked regional government, but felt that existing regions were too large, too arbitrary, too remote from the people. "What I'd like to see", he said, "is a regional government for Lincolnshire".

"Bill", I replied, "You've already got one. It's called the Lincolnshire County Council". ❧❧❧

I am astonished at the way in which socialists — and closet federalists — dismiss the views of ordinary people. Here is a case in point.-

Labour Élitist Derides Ordinary People

On Friday May 12th (2000) I attended the launch meeting of the Europe Committee of the Greater Nottingham Partnership at the Djanoghly Centre for Europe at Nottingham University. The first, keynote speech came from Mr. Chapman, Labour leader on Nottingham City Council, who has clearly bought into the European dream hook, line and sinker.

Three main themes emerged, and without wanting to spoil Mr. Chapman's party, it is worth thinking about them. First of all, he told us how important

Europe was for business and inward investment. Somehow he forgot to mention the recent study by the Institute of Directors, which showed that the net cost to the UK of EU membership was between £15 and £25 billion a year. He forgot to mention the costs of excess European regulation and bureaucracy, estimated at around £10 billion a year. He forgot to mention the looming threat of tax harmonisation, which will be a massive blow to employment, competitiveness and prosperity.

No mention of the End of Life Vehicles Directive, which seems likely to make all European auto companies technically bankrupt. No word of the Tobacco Directive which will cost 200 jobs at Imperial Tobacco in Nottingham. No warning of European energy tax proposals which will drive energy-intensive industries offshore – to countries with lower environmental standards. And nothing about research showing that inward investors come here for low regulation, low taxes, and a business-friendly environment. They rarely mention Europe or the Euro as a reason for investing in the UK.

Then he told us about all the wonderful things that European funding is doing for the region. Now EU funding is around 0.7% of GDP, compared to a figure of around 36% of GDP spent by the UK government, just to get it in perspective. To add to that, a recent study (see my first book "Straight Talking on Europe") shows that every pound we get from Europe costs the British economy around £2.60. They give us back a little of what was our own to start with, they tell us what to do with it, then expect us to be grateful.

Then he went on to tell us that only "the élite" (his word) understood the benefits of Europe, that "ordinary people" still think in stereotypes about straight bananas. Here at last he is half right. The European project has always been driven by élites, by small groups of leaders who are dazzled by the European dream, against a background of indifference or unease from the general public.

Jean Monnet, one of the founding fathers of Europe said, "If we'd told people what we were doing, they'd never have let us do it". In France, the Maastricht Treaty was passed by a cat's whisker. In Denmark, it was lost, so the government told the people they'd have to vote again until they got the right answer. In Germany today, polls show that up to 70% of Germans would like to keep the D-mark. But none of them think they'll be able to. What a travesty of democracy!

We used to think that Labour stood for ordinary people. But Mr. Chapman has let the cat out of the bag. He sees himself as part of an élite that wants to sell Britain down the Euro-river, and he despises the legitimate and genuine concerns of the public. I say thank God for the common sense of ordinary people. As so often happens, they understand the issue better than council leaders or cabinet ministers. ❧❧❧

A response to Tony Blair's Europe speech, November 20th 2001

Blair's Wrong on Europe

On Wednesday November 20th, Prime Minister Tony Blair made a key-note speech at the European Research Institute in Birmingham. He painted a glowing picture of the benefits of EU membership, in terms of peace and prosperity. He argued that Britain had always been a late joiner in European projects, that key decisions were made while we huffed and puffed on the sidelines, that now was the time to get in and take a lead. And he said that Eurosceptics should be embarrassed that all their dire predictions had failed to materialise.

He sounded so plausible. But of course he was wrong from start to finish.

Europe hasn't kept the peace for fifty years. NATO has. Europe hasn't delivered unrivalled prosperity — if anything, the deregulation of global trade through the GATT and later the World Trade Organisation has done that. My own view, reinforced by two years experience in the European parliament, is that European integration represents the greatest threat (short of international terrorism) to our prosperity, to our democracy, and increasingly to our security.

Tony Blair didn't mention the damage that excessive Euro-regulation is doing to our industry. He didn't mention the despair of our farmers and fishermen. He didn't mention the independent estimate from the Institute of Directors that membership of the EU is costing us between £15 and £25 billion a year. No word on the European pensions time-bomb, which means that a vote for the Euro is a vote for higher interest rates, higher taxes, higher unemployment.

He gave us fifty words on the Euro, but he didn't warn us that if we join, the Pound will be scrapped forever, our interest rates and monetary policy will be set by foreign bureaucrats over whom we will have no control at all, and our gold and foreign currency reserves will be trucked to Frankfurt.

Eurosceptics have no reason to be embarrassed at any failed predictions. Let's remember some of the warnings:

The Exchange Rate Mechanism (ERM): We entered the ERM in 1990. All the establishment backed entry — all three major parties, the CBI, the

TUC, the media. Yet the sceptics warned that it would be a disaster. And they were right. We crashed out of the ERM in 1992 on Black Wednesday — September 16th. Millions of jobs lost, thousands of companies bankrupt, hundreds of thousands of families in negative equity, or losing their homes entirely. All because we followed a monetary policy for Europe, instead of a monetary policy for Britain.

The Common Fisheries Policy (CFP): Eurosceptics stated the obvious — that it was lunacy for Britain, with 70% of the EU's fisheries, to give them away. They were right. The CFP has been a disaster for our fishermen — most have had to leave the industry, and once-busy ports are idle. It was a disaster for the housewife. Cod and mackerel used to be cheap. Now they are expensive luxuries. Worst of all, it has been a disaster for the environment, with stocks of key species crashing across the North Sea.

European Legal System: Three years ago I said the time would come when we could be arrested in our home town and shipped abroad to face foreign justice without appeal to our own courts. They said I was scare-mongering. Yet as I write Mr. Blair's government is passing the European Arrest Warrant legislation — which does just what I warned of.

Common Taxation: We warned that despite our tax veto the tax harmonisation agenda would become irresistible, as indeed it has. It is damaging our economy, and costing jobs, *now*. And the Commission is working out clever procedural devices to bypass the member states' vetoes (see Chapter 3)

The Euro: We warned that the Euro would be weak and volatile. It is. We warned that the Euro would be ERM Mark 2. We warned that a one-size-fits-all interest rate would do huge damage. And what do we find? Recession and rising unemployment in Germany, where interest rates are too high. And an unsustainable inflationary boom in Ireland, where interest rates are too low.

The British people are increasingly suspicious of the European project. And as usual, they are right.

Edmund Burke: "Nobody made a greater mistake than he who did nothing because he could do only a little".

Chapter Seven

The War Against Terrorism

As with the assassination of President Kennedy, few of us will ever forget the moment when we heard the news about the World Trade Centre. I was in Brussels, in a no-more-than-ordinarily boring meeting of the industry committee, when an assistant came and whispered in my ear that a plane had crashed into the World Trade Centre. Of course I had no idea that it was a large airliner, packed with passengers and fuel. But I rushed back up to the television in my office, and saw the rest of the tragedy unfold.

The following three pieces were written in the aftermath of those dreadful events.

Time to Fight Back Against Terrorism

Today I have signed the book of condolence which is being prepared by the European parliament and will be presented to the US congress when it is complete. It seems such a small gesture in the face of the monumental tragedy and outrage which has taken place in America, yet it is an important gesture to make. We must do everything we can to show our solidarity with the American people at this dreadful time.

The attacks on the World Trade Centre and the Pentagon are not just attacks on America. They are attacks on all of us. As William Hague put it, "They have declared war on civilisation".

Only a few weeks ago I was in the USA, with a parliamentary delegation, and in the very cities which have been featuring so horribly in the recent news — in Washington, New York, Boston. In fact I have been a regular visitor to the USA since 1972, when I stayed in New York State for three months.

We have an enormous shared heritage with America, and indeed with what Churchill described as "The English Speaking Peoples". Despite the misunderstandings over Suez in the fifties, America has been our closest and most reliable ally for the best part of a century — and we theirs.

Now as the dust settles across Manhattan, the personal stories of courage and agony are coming out. 300 firemen dead. A victim staggering down the stairs at the WTC with not only clothes but skin as well burned off. Brave passengers phoning homes and security forces even as they knew they were bound for death.

For all these reasons, the horror we have seen on our televisions has a special resonance for us. It is impossible to understand the minds of people who would fly an airliner full of innocent people into a building — also full of innocent people. As the Telegraph put it, "Those who claim to commit these acts in the name of Allah, the Compassionate, the Merciful, are blasphemers against their own religion".

NATO was quite right to invoke the treaty clause that makes an attack on one member an attack on all. Freedom is indivisible. And only one country, the USA, has the military and other resources to lead our response. We and our European partners must be prepared to give the Americans our wholehearted support.

The going will get tough. There will be collateral damage. Then the faint-hearts and the appeasers will come out of the woodwork and call for a softer approach. But we have seen in Northern Ireland where that approach takes us. The terrorists will pocket every concession, pounce on every weakness, and then laugh all the way to the conference table. They will give nothing in return. When a terrorist smells weakness, he redoubles his attack.

So we must resolve now, in the aftermath of this appalling atrocity, with the dreadful images still fresh in our minds, that we will go the whole way with our NATO allies, until this threat is contained.

It will mean tighter security, more hassle to get onto an aircraft. And in the end we have to recognise that there is a trade-off between security and freedom. Risk can never be wholly eliminated. But we can and must go after the guilty men and ensure that we leave them unable to repeat the offence.

Tough as we need to be, we must of course remember that not all Arabs, not all Muslims, support the terrorists. In our justified anger, we must not make the mistake of tarring the whole of the Middle East with the same brush. We must hit the target hard, but we must be sure that it is the right target.
᠀᠀᠀᠀

This next article was dated October 3rd — three weeks after the attacks

Blair's Blind Spot

Tony Blair has had a good war so far. He's taken a clear stand against inter-national terrorism. He's flown around the world to help consolidate the alliance against the bombers. He's promised to stand shoulder to shoulder with our American allies, and to provide British forces for the struggle. For all these things I commend him unreservedly.

But as Ulster Unionist leader David Trimble has pointed out, there is a dramatic contradiction between Blair's bold stand against international terrorism, against the evil-doers who committed the dreadful atrocities in the US, and his totally different attitude to domestic terrorism and the IRA. For Tony, terrorists begin at Calais.

In order to keep the pretence of the so-called "Peace Process", Blair is ready to make any concession to the IRA. Convicted terrorists are out of jail and on the streets — some having served only a derisory period inside. Former terrorist leaders become government ministers in Northern Ireland. Blair has kow-towed to the IRA and agreed to knock the stuffing out of the Royal Ulster Constabulary. His reward? Gerry Adam's recent statement that the IRA will treat the new police force as fair game, just as it treated the old one. Woe betide any young Catholic who decides to promote the peace process by joining the police.

On their side, the terrorists make no concessions at all. Rackets and punishment beatings, even shootings and murder, continue. No start has been made on decommissioning. When the terrorists have broken all their previous promises, they just promise again to keep future promises. Their promises are worth nothing. It is time for action.

The IRA pockets every concession, gives nothing in return, and laughs all the way to the conference table.

So what should we do? I offer my suggestion, but I stress that it is my personal view and not Conservative policy. I believe that if we have declared war on international terrorism, it is time to get tough with the IRA. It is time to call their bluff.

Blair should now give them an ultimatum. Either they finish decommissioning — I repeat, finish, not start — by some reasonable date, and to the satisfaction of the British government, say by December 31st. Or else we abandon the failed peace process and adopt a military solution. All the released terrorists go back to jail. All active "Real IRA" members — the security forces know perfectly well who they are and where to find them — are interned. Any terrorist attack or attempt should be treated just as we would treat Osama bin Laden — shoot first and talk afterwards.

Such a course would have been politically and diplomatically unacceptable a few years ago. But two things have changed. First, the world can see that we have bent over backwards to make every possible concession, to coax the IRA into the democratic process. But over and over again they have shown their determination to cling to the terrorist option.

Second, after September 11th and the World Trade Centre, the international attitude to terrorism has hardened. We have had enough. As President Bush has said "We will bring our enemies to justice, or we will bring justice to our enemies. But justice will be done".

I don't ask that Tony Blair should follow my proposal exactly. But I do demand that he get tough with the IRA. Otherwise his bold international stance against terrorism will have feet of clay. ❧❧❧

This next piece followed on October 16th:

Let's Stick to Our Guns!

I have already expressed my support for Tony Blair in his determination to fight terrorism, and to co-operate with our American allies (although I wonder why Tony does so little to fight our home-grown terrorism in Northern Ireland).

But already the voices of appeasement, the faint-hearts and former CND members are out in force, nibbling away at the edges of our commitment. We saw them out marching in European capitals, and also sadly in London as well, at the weekend. They were not in the numbers we saw during the Gulf War, but too many for comfort.

They say they oppose the bombing. So what would they do? Apart from vague appeals to the United Nations, not much. They call for Osama bin Laden to be brought before a court of law, but they don't suggest how we get him there.

I recently heard a spokesman for the Church of Scotland on the radio saying that bombing was wrong, but that it would be alright for snatch squads to go into Afghanistan to arrest bin Laden. The interviewer asked how we could send in snatch squads without first softening up the Afghan defences, and the spokesman replied that he spoke for the church and for morality, he was not a military planner. And a good thing that he is not a military planner, for he clearly had no idea at all of the problems and dangers of sending troops into Afghanistan.

Let's remind ourselves why we are bombing Afghanistan. It is not, absolutely not, for revenge, and it is disgraceful for some commentators to suggest otherwise. It is not to "punish" the terrorists. And still less is it in order to attack Afghan civilians or the Islamic world generally.

Afghanistan is a state that sponsors terrorism, and the links between the Afghan government and bin Laden's Al Qua'ida organisation are so close that it is impossible to deal with them separately. We want to bring bin Laden to justice, along with his henchmen, and to destroy his infrastructure and his training camps. Why? Partly to see justice done. But most importantly to render his organisation incapable of mounting new outrages.

We are not bombing for the sake of bombing. We are bombing as the first stage of a strategy to enable us to destroy this hot-bed of terrorism and hatred, and to make it safe.

Not revenge. Not punishment. Not an attack on Islam. Not solely to see justice done. Overwhelmingly, the reason we are attacking Afghanistan is SELF-DEFENCE. We want to be sure that no more September 11th outrages take place in America — or in the UK, or anywhere.

So let's hang in there. Let's stick to our guns. Let's see the job through to the end. And then let's sleep easy in our beds.

There is a charming little café in the Place Luxembourg on my way into the parliament in Brussels. It's called Le Pain Quotidien — The Daily Bread. I often stop there of a morning for a coffee and croissant. It always used to be 175 Belgian Francs — about £3. Today when I got to the check-out the girl said "Deux cent deux" — 202. "Pourquoi?". I asked in my best French.
"Ah, Monsieur, c'est le Euro", she said.
I make that an increase of about 15%. But it comes out nicely to 5 Euros. So beware the hidden costs of rounding-up!
RFH

Chapter Eight

Race, Immigration and Asylum

The issue of race, asylum and immigration has never been far from the headlines during my years in the European Parliament. The hideous brigades of the politically-correct seem determined to close down any serious debate, and to deny the common-sense views of ordinary people, while at the same time promoting policies that enhance a sense of grievance among minority groups, and promote the race relations industry, which many believe does more harm than good. I first wrote about the issue in May 2000.

Asylum Seekers – Time for Action

After Dover, the preferred port of entry for asylum seekers, Northampton has one of the worst asylum problems in the country. Different reasons are advanced for this. It may be that Northampton is the first truck-stop for incoming lorries after Dover. It may just be that asylum seekers, reasonably enough, like to be with their friends and relatives, so that any concentration of them naturally grows.

Whatever the reason, the problem is real enough. Young men loiter in shopping malls, crime levels rise, the costs to Northamptonshire are reckoned in seven figures and must eventually result in reduced services, or increased council tax, or both.

Let's be clear on one point to start with. This is a social problem that has nothing whatever to do with racism – although too many politicians are prepared to shout racism in an attempt to stifle debate. The fact is that most of the current wave of asylum seekers are white Europeans, so the issue of racism doesn't arise. The plain fact is that regardless of race, our small island cannot cope with tens of thousands of economic migrants, and there is no reason why it should. Of course we want to provide asylum, as we always have, for those suffering real persecution, but all the evidence is that even on very generous criteria, four out of five asylum seekers are bogus – and I don't apologise for the word bogus. Let's address the problem in plain English.

People who really care about race relations in the UK know that excessive immigration is likely to create negative feelings against minorities, and that proper immigration controls are essential to maintain our generally good record on race relations in this country.

The truth is that Labour have made Britain a soft touch for asylum seekers. They delayed checks on illegal employment, they reversed high-profile deportation decisions, they declared an amnesty for illegal immigrants. Why else would migrants from Eastern Europe travel through Austria and Germany and Belgium and France, and only think to claim asylum when they get to the UK?

The government is taking months or years to process asylum seekers, and even the majority of applications, which are refused, don't result in deportation – the asylum seekers have slipped away into the community, to await the next amnesty.

So what's to be done? The Conservative Party says, first of all, no more amnesties. Asylum seekers should be detained until their cases are heard, and deported if not successful. I would go further. Asylum seekers coming most recently from France (as most of them do) should be sent back the same day they arrive, and told to seek asylum in France. We must re-establish the "white list" of safe countries, where human rights are respected and the rule of law prevails, and nationals of those countries should not be entitled to claim asylum.

That raises a key question about the Eastern European countries applying to join the EU. To be eligible to become applicant nations, they must meet basic human rights criteria. They can't have it both ways. Either they don't respect human rights, in which case the EU would not have accepted their candidacy, or they do, in which case their nationals cannot claim political asylum.

There are six billion people in the world, most of whom are much poorer that we in the UK. We simply can't accept them all here, or even a significant proportion of them. The rule must be – genuine asylum seekers yes, economic migrants, no. ༄༅༄༅

I returned to the subject in April 2001

Race, Immigration and Asylum

Last weekend I appeared on ITV's "It's Your Shout" programme, and I was asked straight out whether I would sign the Commission for Racial Equality's famous declaration on racism. Knowing that politicians should never give straight answers to straight questions, I replied "No, I would not" (although of course as a Euro-MP, I am not a candidate in the general election, so the CRE has not invited me to sign).
So why not? The declaration itself is fine. Indeed it is against the law to stir

up racial hatred, so all the CRE is really doing is to ask people to sign a paper saying they'll keep to the law – as if they'd asked us to promise not to commit larceny or murder. I am very happy that William Hague has signed on behalf of the Conservative party.

But as John Gummer said very forcefully on the Today programme recently, I believe that individual parliamentarians should speak to their constituents and the media in their own words, not just sign up parrot-like to every statement from every pressure group. And we get a lot. Frequently I agree with them. For example, many politicians recently received a strongly Euro-sceptic manifesto, the South Molton Declaration, and were invited to sign it. I agreed with it, but I preferred not to sign up to someone else's manifesto.

There is something rather sinister and McCarthyite about a government-sponsored quango asking opposition politicians to sign their statement, and making veiled threats of naming and shaming for those who won't sign. The whole thing looks rather like an elephant trap designed by the Labour Party and the CRE to trap the Tories – but we're not going to be trapped.

I shall avoid racist comments — firstly, because that's the right thing to do and I don't want to make racist comments to start with (and it's insulting to candidates for the CRE to suggest otherwise); secondly because it's the law; and thirdly because William Hague has committed the party to the CRE declaration, and I am happy and proud to follow William's lead.

There remains the question of who is to be the judge of racist comments. Both Labour politicians, like Robin Cook in his Chicken Tikka Masala speech, and Lib-Dems like Charles Kennedy, have chosen to shout "racist" whenever we Tories dare to mention asylum and immigration. Indeed it seems to me that their unfounded accusations amount to playing the race card and to breaking the declaration which they have signed.

They have argued that William Hague's famous "foreign land" speech was racist, when everyone who heard it knows perfectly well that he was referring to the way Labour are handing powers to Brussels and turning our country into an off-shore province in the Euro-super-state. He wasn't talking about immigration or asylum at all.

I have already written to Mr. Gorbbux Singh, Chairman of the CRE, asking him to investigate these statements by Cook and Kennedy to see if he agrees that they have broken their commitments.

Which would you rather have? A Tory who won't sign but keeps the terms, or a Labour or Lib-Dem politician who signs and then breaks the terms?

The fact is that most of the bogus asylum seekers arriving at Dover are white Europeans, so the question of racism doesn't arise. The issue is not about race. It's about raw numbers, about pressures on society and infrastructure, about costs imposed on local authorities and ratepayers. This is a big issue on the doorstep with all kinds of voters, including ethnic minorities.

The government knows the public are worried about immigration, and they are desperate to stop the Tories talking about Labour's massive failures in this area. They're trying to intimidate us by shouting "racist" whenever we mention these subjects. But I have bad news for Robin Cook. We won't be intimidated. This is a legitimate area of public concern. It is a key area of government failure. And it will be a key issue in the election. ₂₂₂

The cynical and opportunist use of the race issue by the left was rarely better illustrated than by the use they made of it during the Conservative leadership campaign in 2001.

Race and Repatriation

Curious — and a gift to the Labour Party — that the issue of race raised its head, repeatedly, during the Conservative leadership contest. Let's be clear about this. Any large organisation (there are over 300,000 members of the Tory party) will include individuals who have unacceptable racist views. But as a party, we resolutely reject racism. And we recognise that we have a great deal more work to do to ensure that more members of ethnic minorities get into Westminster and other elected offices.

Here in the European parliament, two out of our 35 members are from ethnic minorities. We'd like to see more — and more women — but it's a start. We certainly need a culture change throughout the party so that selection committees are more positive about women and minorities.

But I was surprised by the vehemence with which some party spokesmen attacked the concept of voluntary repatriation. It was described in the most intemperate language — "abhorrent" was one of the milder words used.

I have even seen the idea of voluntary repatriation compared to ethnic cleansing. This is a lunatic comparison. Ethnic cleansing means forcing people from their homes against their will. It's just about the opposite of voluntary repatriation, just as charity is nearly the opposite of theft, and health care is nearly the opposite of murder.

Let's think what we mean by voluntary repatriation. Imagine an immigrant family — perhaps from the Caribbean or South Asia — who come to Britain with high hopes, but find after a year or two that things are not working out, they miss their homeland, their extended family, perhaps even the sunshine of their birthplace. But imagine that they don't have the money for the ticket home.

What do we say to them? "Sorry, chaps, you have to stay whether you like it or not"? Or do we say "We'll help you to do what you want to do"? It seems to me both generous and humane that we should help them. It's a win-win deal. We in Britain don't want to keep immigrant families here against their will, and they don't want to stay.

If voluntary repatriation is "abhorrent" and "right-wing", it's curious to reflect that it was introduced in the 1971 Immigration Act by the Heath government (Section 29), and it remains in force today under a Labour government. In fact last year the Labour government allowed £120,000 of public funds for exactly this purpose. A similar scheme operates in France where it was introduced by a socialist government. Voluntary repatriation was supported by the late left-wing black MP Bernie Grant — hardly the man to support an abhorrent, right-wing racist policy.

The Tory Party was right to throw out the Welshman Mr. Griffin. But in my view, the reason for sacking him was his links with the BNP — a party with totally unacceptable racist views. I do not think that it would have been right to sack him for supporting voluntary repatriation, and I believe that many if not most Conservatives would agree that voluntary repatriation is a common sense solution to a genuine problem.

Racism is wrong. All British subjects should be treated equally under the law, and by their neighbours and fellow citizens. But voluntary repatriation has been in place for thirty years, it is a generous, humane solution for those who freely and of their own volition, choose to return to their country of origin. We need a little less excitement and rhetoric, and a little more common sense.

ᢒᥱᢒᥱᢒᥱᢒᥱ

> *"In political terms, the Channel is wider than the Atlantic"*
> *– Lord Shore of Stepney*
> *(the late Peter Shore, former Labour cabinet minister)*

Chapter Nine

International Trade: Does the EU Help?

Much of the debate about Britain's status in the EU revolves around the question of international trade. It tends to be assumed, without evidence or debate, that EU member-ship is self-evidently good for British trade. That view is open to question.

The EU Single Market: Better for the USA than the UK?

During the 1999 European election campaign, a colleague came to me with a problem. She'd given a robust Euro-sceptic speech, but was stumped when a questioner said "So why are we in the EU anyway?" Of course I had the usual glib answer: "Single Market – great Conservative achievement".

More recently, I made a dismissive remark on a TV show about "the benefits of EU membership", and I was berated by a Tory MEP colleague who warned me never to disparage the benefits of the Single Market. Meantime senior Tory spokesmen speak unthinkingly of "the undoubted benefits to Britain of EU membership" – which they seldom enumerate.

This started me thinking, and I reached two startling and counter-intuitive conclusions. First, although there are real benefits for Britain from the Single Market, those benefits are clearly outweighed by the costs of regulation. And second, that non-member states who trade with the EU – the USA, China, Japan, Norway – actually derive **more** benefit from the EU's Single Market than we do.

The Institute of Directors (IoD) produced a policy paper in March 2000, which states that the current net cost of UK membership of the EU is at least £15 billion per annum. In arriving at this figure, the IoD generously assumes that there is a benefit from FDI – inward foreign direct investment into the UK – equivalent to 0.5% of GDP per annum, compared to not being in the EU. However the IoD points out that another FDI scenario is plausible: that in a UK outside the EU, British business would have a lower cost and regulatory burden and therefore attract **more** inward investment compared to being in the EU. Under this scenario, the annual cost of membership could (compared to being outside) increase to £25 billion or 0.8% of GDP – more than we spend each year on defence. And tax harmonisation could double that again.

Non-member states like the USA have good access to the Single Market, but avoid the EU's regulatory burdens. Figures published by the think-tank

"Global Britain" show that US merchandise exports to the EU grew faster over 1992/98 than the UK's exports to the rest of the EU – at 4.5% per annum compared to 3.6%. And UK exports to non-EU countries are growing faster than exports within the EU.

Global Britain point out in their Fortnightly Briefing, 3rd March 2000, that the cost to the US economy of tariffs into the EU was significantly less, in percentage terms, than the direct net cost to the UK economy of British EU membership, expressed as a percentage of our merchandise exports to the EU. Meantime the recent EU/ Mexico free trade agreement gives Mexico all the benefits of the Single Market and none of the costs. Well done Mexico!

We are told that the Single Market, by creating a great, border-less market with common standards and specifications, gives massive advantages, and means we can compete with the USA on level terms. But the analysis by Patrick Minford and Bill Jamieson, *"Britain and Europe: Choices for Change"* clearly shows that European growth falls far behind that of the powerhouse US economy, to the extent that the size of the US economy will double relative to Europe over the next 25 years.

A key explanation for this dramatic difference in performance is the huge regulatory burden in the EU, with its sclerotic labour markets. These are well documented, and despite my best efforts on the European parliament's Environment and Employment committees, the situation gets worse by the day. Chronic high levels of unemployment are a further symptom of the problem.

The question arises: do the benefits of the Single Market necessarily depend on the massive, oppressive and heavy-handed regulatory and institutional structures of the EU? Clearly not. It is an exaggeration (but not a huge one) to say that for all practical purposes the whole mountain of EU regulation could be replaced by a dozen words. We simply need to state that all products and services which are legal in one member state are legal in all – mutual recognition rather than common regulation. Such an EU would deliver the essential benefits of the Single Market. It would require the Council of Ministers, and perhaps a limited disputes resolution procedure, but it would not need the Commission, the Parliament, the European Court of Justice or the European Central Bank.

EU apologists point to a recent up-turn in growth, and slight dip in continental unemployment, as evidence of a turn-around, some citing "the success of the Euro" as the reason. In fact of course, it is the *failure* of the Euro, and its massive devaluation, which have resulted in short-term export-led blip in European economic performance. But we in the UK of all people should know that the economic benefits of devaluation are fool's gold.

So for member states, the benefits of the Single Market are lost in the morass of the EU social model. But of course, third countries which trade with the EU get all the benefits of this vast consumer market, without the ball-and-chain of EU regulation. The Single Market delivers its benefits undiluted to external trading partners like Norway and the USA.

If you follow this analysis, you might rush to the conclusion that Britain would be better off out, and I would be hard-pressed to disagree. But the ideal solution – the solution espoused by the Tory party – is to change the EU, or at least our relationship with it, from within, in such a way as to get the benefits without the costs. But if those attempts fail, the fallback position of withdrawal looks increasingly attractive. ❧❧❧

In October 2000, I was prompted by a speech by Tony Blair to address the issue of the supposed "isolation" that Britain would suffer without the EU.

Britain: Greater Than You Realised?

Several times recently, East Midlands constituents have said to me, more or less, "Look, Britain's finished. Most of our businesses and famous name firms have been bought up by foreigners. The only new jobs are created by the Japanese. We may as well give up".

They are astonished when I explain to them how false this view is. It's true that some of our great companies have been bought by foreigners, but far more of **their** companies have been bought by **us**. It's a two-way trade where Britain is winning handsomely. In fact, Britain is the world's second largest global investor after the USA – bigger than Germany or France. Nearly three quarters of our overseas investments are outside Euroland. And incidentally, far more of our inward investment comes from the USA than from Japan.

In fact both our trade and our massive overseas investments are much more outside Europe – much more global – than those of our EU partners. This fact by itself is enough reason for Britain to keep the Pound. Everyone recognises that joining the Euro requires convergence, but the pattern of our trade and investments shows no sign of convergence – indeed the opposite.

A new UN report on Foreign Direct Investment (FDI) gives the lie to those who say that we will lose inward investment outside Euroland. Exactly the opposite is proving to be the case. In 1999, the first full year of the Euro, FDI in Euroland went down 2%. But in the three non-Euro EU countries, Britain, Sweden & Denmark, it increased 66%! Little Sweden actually attracted more FDI in 1999 than the much bigger economies of France or Germany! This shows that financial markets are giving the Euro the thumbs-down. They choose to invest in non-Euro countries because they can see that our economic prospects are better outside the Euro.

And in 1999, Britain was actually the world's Number One global investor, even ahead of the USA!

Now Tony Blair has made a major speech in Poland calling for Europe to be "A super-power not a super-state". As with so much that Tony says, this sounds good but has no meaning. He's playing word-games. How can you have a super-power that is not a super-state?

He offers Britain a false choice. Either we can be leaders at the heart of Europe, he says, or we can be "isolated and marginalised".

Prime Minister after Prime Minister has sought to lead in Europe, and it always ends in tears. Why? Because our partners agree with each other about the European social model of high tax, high spending and high regulation. We on the other hand prefer the Anglo-Saxon model of less government, less tax, less regulation. It's one against fourteen. So we shall never win the arguments in Europe. The best we shall get is a murky compromise that leaves us worse off than we were before.

And it's a very strange kind of isolation that Tony Blair threatens us with. We trade globally with Europe, America, Asia. We are the world's second biggest investor and fourth biggest economy. We have the best armed forces in Europe. We are members of the UN Security Council, NATO, the G7, the World Bank, the IMF, the OECD. We are the leading member of the Commonwealth. Come on, Tony, what sort of isolation is that?

As William Hague rightly said, the only way that Britain could become isolated and marginalised would be to become an offshore province in a European super-state.

The real choice facing Britain is between remaining a great, proud, free, independent sovereign nation, governed democratically from Westminster, engaged with Europe but not run by Brussels, or becoming absorbed in a profoundly anti-democratic European super-state, run by unelected, unaccountable and unsackable bureaucrats.

It is a choice between a great rôle and a global future, or becoming a mere province in the most over-taxed, over-borrowed, over-governed and over-regulated bloc in the world.

Tony Blair lacks the vision and the guts to deliver an open, flexible, democratic, free-trading Europe. We need a Prime Minister who understands the problem and is determined to deliver the solution. A Conservative Prime Minister.

৵৶৶৶

Robin Cook's Unethical Statistics

Former Foreign Minister Robin Cook was the founder (and the gravedigger!) of the government's so-called "ethical foreign policy". He was, and remains, a great advocate of the Euro. And he is constantly going about claiming that Europe accounts for 60% of our overseas trade.

A new study gives the lie to Mr. Cook's figures. They are so misleading as to be downright deceitful. The study is written and researched by a hot-shot city economist, Roger Bootle, formerly Chief Economist with the bank HSBC, and now head of his own consultancy Capital Economics. It is published by the NO campaign, a joint venture between Business for Sterling and Lord Owen's "New Europe" group. Their slogan is "Europe Yes. Euro No".

Of course trade statistics are notoriously ambiguous. Do we mean imports, exports or both? Just goods, or do we include services (which are increasing in importance — financial services, intellectual property, tourism)? What about investment income and other transfers? Does Europe mean the Euro zone (twelve countries), or the EU (fifteen countries) or the whole continent (dozens of countries)? Do we choose just one year, where a random fluctuation may give a freak result, or do we take an average?

Bootle has looked at a statistic called the Current Account, which includes goods, services and investment income. And he has taken it from 1990 to 1999 (the latest full year for which full statistics are available). He focuses on the Euro zone, because after all that's what we're being invited to join.

His conclusion is that Eurozone trade is only 43% of the total, and we trade more with America than with France and Germany combined. Only 19% of our goods exports are invoiced in Eurozone currencies, while 27% are invoiced in dollars.

Looking more broadly at currency areas, and including the economic zones of each major currency, he concludes that the US dollar is actually much more important for Britain's trade and global investments than the Euro. This supports a point I have been making for years: that we don't want to give up the Pound at all, but that if we did, we'd be better off joining a strong Dollar than a sickly Euro.

Looking ahead and taking into account the declining population trends in the EU countries, Bootle concludes that over the first half of the 21st century the EU will actually decline as a proportion of UK trade, and the rest of the world will increase.

Cook and his colleagues argue that 3½ million British jobs depend on trade with the EU. That may be so, but you don't have to join the Euro in order to trade. Millions of jobs in the USA, in China and Japan depend on EU trade, but they're not applying to join the Euro. In fact in the last ten years US trade with the EU has grown faster than our own — you don't have to be in the club to trade with it.

They promised us that the Euro would be strong and stable. In fact it's been weak and volatile. We can already see the damage that a one-size-fits-all interest rate is doing in Germany — where it's too high and is stunting growth — and in Ireland — where it's too low and is fuelling inflation.

Many people in the East Midlands may not realise that joining the Euro means **scrapping the Pound** — forever — and sending our gold and foreign currency reserves to the European Central Bank in Frankfurt. When they understand these points, up to 90% of the British people oppose the Euro.

Only one country in the EU has voted on the Euro — Denmark — and they voted NO. Thank heavens that John Major negotiated a Euro opt-out at Maastricht, so at least we have a choice. Britain is the world's fourth largest economy and second largest global investor. We are much better managing our own currency and setting our own monetary policy for our own economy, than farming it out to foreign bureaucrats in Frankfurt. ❧

"Britain's Trade with the EU and the rest of the world: what does our current account really look like?". By Roger Bootle. Published at £5 by The NO Campaign, 56 Ayres St., London SE1 1EU, Phone 020 7378 0436.

Most of us were shocked by the antics of the so-called anti-globalisation protesters at Seattle and elsewhere. I addressed the topic on May 2nd, 2001.

May-Day Madness

Back in 1988 I was running a textile company in Malaysia, in the small town of Malacca on the west coast. The company was part of a multinational textile group – the sort of company that May-Day's anti-capitalist demonstrators are opposed to. I was asked by the group to take responsibility for the start-up of a new subsidiary in Vietnam, on the outskirts of Saigon. This was in addition to the day job, and the Malacca company was responsible for hiring and training Vietnamese nationals to staff the new business.

I made many visits to Saigon, and one to Hanoi. In those days, before my knees gave up, I was a bit of a runner, and I would always go out running before breakfast in a new city. Vietnam in those days had only just opened to the world. There were few motor vehicles, but huge numbers of bicycles.

I remember one morning I was running down the street surrounded by bicycles – we all seemed to be going at about the same speed – and I was suddenly struck by the appalling poverty of the people. What on earth could I do, I thought, to help them? Then it occurred to me that by going to Vietnam, opening a textile factory, training and employing staff, I was already doing the very best thing for them – far better than foreign aid and handouts. I was giving them the means, the capital and the skills to earn their own living and to take pride in their achievements.

So when our May-Day protesters say they're against capitalism and globalisation and privatisation, it seems to me that they're actually against prosperity and jobs. Their policies (if indeed they have any policies beyond anarchy and nihilism) would condemn poor people to more poverty, and deny them the opportunity to work their way to prosperity.

As President George W. Bush has pointed out, free trade not only creates wealth. It also tends to go hand-in-hand with political freedom. Closed economies and closed markets foster closed countries and closed minds.

Of course capitalism and free markets are far from perfect – what system is not? Poverty and inequality remain, as a challenge for policymakers. But much of the world's poverty results not from globalisation but from the lack of democratic institutions. Sub-Saharan Africa is often described as a basket-case, and Robert Mugabe's Zimbabwe (or Southern Rhodesia, as I still think of it) illustrates why. It could be – it was – a prosperous country, but the breakdown of civil institutions and the rule of law is decimating its economy.

At the World Conference on Racism and Xenophobia, Lib-Dem MEP Baroness Ludford has tabled a motion condemning colonialism and its legacy. Certainly Zimbabwe is not much of an advertisement for the colonial legacy – one man, one vote, one President. But other countries fared better. I spent a total of five years in Singapore and Malaysia, where the legacy of British rule is mostly positive. Democratic institutions, the rule of law, infrastructure, education, health. These countries have made great strides since independence, but we left them a firm foundation on which to build. India, the world's largest democracy, might never have existed as an entity without British rule.

Like capitalism, Britain's colonial history was not all good, and there were events and incidents that we could never justify, least of all by today's politically-correct standards. But on the whole I believe that the British people should be proud of what the Empire achieved. I wish that Lib-Dem MEPs could take a balanced view, and not simply focus on the bad and ignore the good.

As for the May-Day protesters, they say, amazingly, that they believe in democracy but are forced onto the streets because no political party promotes their policies. They could start by telling us what their policies are, if any. And they should remember that we already have a democracy. All they need to do is to put up candidates and convince us to vote for them. *≈*≈*≈*

In April 2000 I was struck by a curious international trade anomaly — that Mexico could benefit from free trade with the EU without the massive drawbacks of European regulation and the European social model. I wrote to the Daily Telegraph about it.

The Editor,   6 April, 2000
The Daily Telegraph,
1 Canada Square,
London E14 5DT
Fax: 0044 20 7538 5000

Dear Sir,

The EU is concluding a free trade agreement with Mexico. The question arises: if Mexico, a member of NAFTA, can have a free trade agreement with the EU, why cannot the UK, a member of the EU, have a free trade agreement with NAFTA?

The technical answer to this conundrum is simple: NAFTA is a free trade area, whereas the EU is a customs union. However it begs a deeper question: is it in Britain's interests to be a member of a customs union? Customs unions are past their sell-by date in the twenty-first century. The Conservative Party should press for treaty changes to enable the EU to turn itself into a free trade area.

Then we could conclude a free trade agreement with NAFTA, with or without our EU partners.

Yours faithfully,

ROGER HELMER MEP

Chapter Ten

Over-regulation in the EU

When I speak to businesses in the East Midlands, their first concern is usually the dreadful burden of excessive EU regulation — closely followed by a well-founded fear that we in Britain "gold-plate" European legislation and enforce it far too rigorously, creating an enormous competitive disadvantage for our industry. It is a problem I have returned to many times. And I spend a great deal of time in the European parliament arguing and voting against excessive and damaging regulation.

The first piece comes from February 2000

Bad Law – and Too Much of It!

If you knew a manufacturer who shifted production back and forth every month between two factories three hundred miles apart, you'd think he was daft – and you'd be right. Yet this is what the European Parliament does, and you pay the costs of it. Despite constant efforts by MEPs to stop it, the French have a veto and we can't change it.

And the European Parliament IS a factory – a factory that churns out huge quantities of legislation, regulation and directives, most of them bad, most of them ill-considered. Some examples:

Last week we passed the "End of Life Vehicles Directive". This will place a huge financial burden on Europe's car manufacturers. It will damage competitiveness and prosperity in Europe, and it will cost jobs. As I said at a meeting of the full parliament last week, "In this Parliament we constantly talk about the need to cut unemployment, yet we pass directives like this one which will cost jobs".

It is anti-competitive, favouring new Asian car suppliers against established European car-makers, who have more vehicles out there on the road. And it isn't even very good for the environment, because it prescribes one particular method of recycling which may not be the best environmentally, and certainly isn't cost-effective. Tory MEPs voted against, but it went through.

Then there was the Water Framework Directive. We needed to make a vital decision on how quickly to introduce the new measures. The decision required a highly technical analysis of costs and benefits for the two proposed time-scales, but we ended up with a sterile debate between eco-warriors saying "Sooner", and more business-friendly MEPs saying "Later". Neither side had enough technical knowledge to justify its position.

Suddenly out of the woodwork a couple of weeks ago emerged a proposal called the "Tobin tax". This is a proposal for a tax on capital movements in Europe. Boring and technical, but if the so-called withholding tax was like shooting ourselves in the foot, then the Tobin tax was shooting ourselves in the head. We defeated it by half a dozen votes. Some of my colleagues were elated that we'd won. I was deeply discouraged at the thought that very nearly half the MEPs had voted for such a mad idea.

Then we have the so-called "Charter of Fundamental Rights", as if we didn't have enough "Rights", with the UN Declaration and the European Convention. The hidden agenda with this new Charter is to create a constitution for a single state of Europe. It will radically change our legal system – suddenly all decisions will be made by reference to this arbitrary socialist Charter, and the basis of our common law and precedent will have gone. As MEPs, we get the chance to tinker with the idea at the edges, but no effective opportunity to vote against the whole thing, lock, stock and barrel.

Then there are the proposals for the Inter-Governmental Conference later this year, leading to a new Treaty of Nice (following on from Amsterdam and Maastricht). This will turn the integrationist screw a little tighter, and bring political union in Europe closer.

So does nothing good come out of the European Parliament? Occasionally it does. The Single Market in Financial Services, for example, would be good for Britain, good for European investors, good for European industry. But the French and Germans are threatening to hold it up unless we cave in on their mad withholding tax. The benefits that might be achieved are horse-traded away.

Conservative MEPs will continue to fight for Britain's interests and resist daft and damaging proposals. But we should understand that the cards are stacked against us. We won't win in the European game until we have a Tory government in Westminster determined to stop the rot. ❧❧❧

The Tobacco Directive was promoted as a health measure — although its shaky legal basis was the Single Market legislation. In this piece, I argue that it did little or nothing either for health or for the single market. What it did was to damage European industry and cost jobs.

EU Tobacco Directive: a Lose-lose Deal

The European Union's new Tobacco Directive, due for its second reading in Strasbourg later this year (2000), is deeply flawed. It is intellectually confused. It will do little or nothing to protect the public, but it will do significant economic damage to the EU.

Let me start with a disclaimer. I have been a lapsed smoker for twenty-five years, and I hate smoking with all the zeal of a convert. I have been known to go around the European Parliament putting paper bags on the heads of smokers in non-smoking areas. Nevertheless, dislike of smoking is no excuse for badly drafted legislation, and I shall be voting against the Directive, for the second time, next month.

The Directive will mandate lower tar, nicotine and carbon monoxide levels for cigarettes sold in the EU. Reduced tar and nicotine have been central to regulatory efforts for twenty-five years. Manufacturers have been pressured by lawmakers to lower the strength of cigarettes, and to promote "mild" and "lite" brands.

There is now, however, increasing doubt about the validity of this approach. Recent research shows that smokers switching to milder cigarettes may smoke more cigarettes, may smoke each cigarette further down its length, and critically may start to inhale more deeply to get the same nicotine fix. Cigarette smokers, especially young women who favour mild cigarettes, are presenting with new, deep-lung cancers.

There is a further reason to doubt the wisdom of mild cigarettes. If the manufacturers were setting out to design a cigarette which would be particularly attractive and accessible to young smokers and new smokers, what better than a mild cigarette? Certainly most youngsters would be put off by Capstan Full Strength. By mandating mild cigarettes, we are actually helping the industry to recruit new, young smokers.

The EU appears in part to recognise this danger. The Directive proposes to outlaw the use of the descriptors "Mild" and "Lite", on the grounds that these may give false impression of safety – despite the fact that the EU, and the industry, have been promoting mild cigarettes for decades. But one of two things must be true. Either mild cigarettes are safer, or they are not. If they are safer, why ban the descriptors? And if not, why ban regular-strength cigarettes?

The move to milder cigarettes in the EU, however, is only half of the problem. Extraordinarily, the Directive will also ban the **export** of all but mild cigarettes. Extraordinary first because the legal basis of the Directive is the Single Market and no one can explain how an export ban improves the functioning of the Single Market. Extraordinary secondly because the measure will have no health impact at all – manufacture will simply be switched outside the EU – and yet thousands of jobs will be destroyed, 200 in my own East Midlands constituency in the UK.

It is estimated that 1,800 jobs are directly at risk in the UK, but that number increases to 8,300 if we include jobs in the industry's supply chain. The corresponding figures for the EU as a whole could be as high as 9,500 jobs in the industry and 30,000 in total. Most of the non-UK manufacture is in Germany.

Despite the legal basis of the directive, the EU institutions invoke a public health argument against exports. They say that it would be morally reprehensible to allow the export to third countries of dangerous cigarettes which are banned in the EU. Never mind that there are many cases, for example in chemicals and agricultural products, where goods which are not legal in the EU are freely exported to third countries. Never mind that smokers in Asia and Africa and South America will continue to smoke their preferred cigarettes – the product will simply be made in Bangkok or Bangladesh or Buenos Aires, instead of in the EU.

There will be no health dividend at all. And yet sanctimonious MEPs and Commission officials strike moral postures about the export of "dangerous products", with no regard at all to the jobs and families and mortgages of workers in the industry. As so often happens, the European parliament talks earnestly about the need to reduce unemployment, and then passes a measure to export jobs.

The outright hypocrisy of this position is highlighted by the subsidies of well over half a billion dollars a year which the EU gives to support tobacco production in Greece and Italy. The tobacco produced in these countries is of such execrable quality that no one in the EU wants it, and it has to exported to the third world. The pious MEPs who throw thousands of European tobacco workers to the wolves without a second thought, on the grounds of "morality", are the same MEPs who vote massive subsidies for exports of bad tobacco to the third world.

There is a deeply dangerous precedent here. In the overall scheme of things, the transfer of cigarette manufacture offshore may not be a body-blow to the EU economy. But if we decide to ban the export of all products which are banned for sale within the EU, the economic damage could be significant. It is a fundamental principle of international trade that exporters should design products to meet the legislation and consumer preferences of their target market. If they must also meet the legislation of their home market on export products, great swathes of international business will be abandoned to non-EU countries.

The Tobacco Directive is unnecessary. It is pious and sanctimonious. It is pointless and damaging. It is political correctness run mad. It is designed to support the moral posturing of legislators, not the needs of the European economy or European consumers. It should be rejected.   ❧❧❧

This piece from February 2001 was prompted by comments from the many companies I visit across the East Midlands

Catch Them Doing Something Right!

Years ago a business colleague gave me an excellent piece of advice in dealing with staff. " Try to catch them doing something **right**" he said. Often a word of praise is worth a yard of criticism. But it's a message that Britain's growing army of inspectors hasn't learnt.

And how the army grows! Recently a member of the public said to William Hague: "You know if we go on like this, Mr. Hague, we'll soon have one bloke working in this country and fifty million blokes watching him".

A businessman who operates both in the UK and on the Continent recently said to me: "I have the impression that inspectors on the continent regard themselves as partners who try to help companies to operate within the rules, whereas in Britain they merely want to catch you out and stop you doing things".

Another said "The inspectors from the Environment Agency used to be mature people with production experience. They'd go out on the site and see what was going on. But now we get young graduates with no understanding of the industry, but with zealous anti-business attitudes. They don't want to go on-site or get their hands dirty, they just want mountains of reports".

In the last couple of years I have visited literally hundreds of businesses, large and small, up and down the East Midlands. Without a doubt, the biggest concern they have is excessive regulation – most of it from Europe. We have the working time directive and the minimum wage, which make very little difference to most workers (most companies were already paying over the minimum wage, and large numbers of workers have opted out of the working time directive), but which add heavy administrative burdens to business.

Every aspect of a company's operations is tied up in red tape. Much of it is well-intentioned but ineffective or counter-productive. Europe's recent "Rickety Ladders Directive" is a case in point. We all want safety, but massive Euro-directives are not the way to achieve it. If you showed your window-cleaner a fat EU directive on how to use a ladder, he wouldn't know whether to laugh or cry.

Meantime the government tries to turn companies into unpaid tax inspectors with measures like the "Working Family Tax Credit".

But it is the differential, over-zealous application of European directives which perhaps does most to damage British competitiveness. Four examples:

Britain has nearly a hundred times as many factory inspectors as Italy – a country of similar size. Guess which country has the toughest enforcement!

I was recently at a plant in Lincolnshire making potato-grading equipment. Under EU rules, this should have an infra-red cut-out to turn it off if the operator reaches inside. The company exhibited at French agricultural shows, but couldn't compete on price with local equipment – which lacked the infra-red safety device. "We know about the rules", said the French suppliers, "but our customers won't pay for the safety cut-out, so we don't fit it".

The famous game dealer Skidmores in Bakewell used to display game outside his shop window. It was an attractive feature of this tourist town. But then along came the health and safety inspector and banned the display under EU hygiene rules. Yet anyone who travels in Europe knows that such displays are commonplace in continental markets.

An EU directive requires fork-lift trucks to be checked regularly for safety. But when drafted into national laws, "regularly" means monthly in the UK, annually in Italy. So much for a level playing field!

How do we sort out the mess? There are several things we need to do. First, we need a government in Westminster that will turn off the regulatory tap – and that means a Tory government. We need proper regulatory impact assessments on new legislative proposals – I have been pressing for this in the European parliament. We need to convince Westminster politicians and civil servants to stop gold-plating regulations. And we must convince our army of inspectors to see themselves as partners of industry, to "catch them doing something right". ❧❧❧

From late on in 2001 comes the European Commission proposal for a new chemicals testing régime — which looks set to result in millions of animals being unnecessarily tested

Millions of Animals at Risk

A new EU proposal, on the testing of chemical, risks doing huge damage to industry — and massively increasing the amount of testing we do on animals. Millions of animals are at risk.

The EU Commission has recognised that around 30,000 chemical substances in common use have never been tested, and they are arguing that tests should now be carried out, on the so-called "precautionary principle". That is, if there is any conceivable risk, we should check it out. Amendments tabled by the Parliament would increase the number of chemicals to 100,000.

So far, so good, you might say. By all means let's minimise risk. But many of these chemical products have been in use for years, or even decades, without the merest hint of any problems.

There are two key areas of concern. The first is that the huge costs of testing and compliance will force many perfectly safe substances off the market. They may be entirely harmless, but the costs of the testing procedure will be unsustainable. This could cause not only the withdrawal of useful products, but huge damage to businesses, including small businesses, and job losses. There are real socio-economic costs here, and they have not been properly considered.

The second issue is the method of testing. The Commission admits that many millions of animals could be subjected to laboratory testing. These tests in my opinion are largely unnecessary.

I am not a fundamentalist on animal testing. There are some areas, especially in the development of new drugs, where animal testing is still necessary. Better to test a new drug on a mouse than a man — or a woman. But we should minimise both the extent of testing and the discomfort of the animals. I am simply appalled that an arbitrary and ill-thought-out piece of legislation should threaten literally millions of animals with unnecessary suffering.

British Tories will be voting against this outrageous proposal. What should we do instead? First of all we should look at the 100,000 chemicals and decide which ones might be dangerous, taking into account the past history of safe use. Second, many of these substances are closely related. It may be sufficient to test just one example from a family of substances. Third, we should look at international experience, and accept the results of tests that have already been done elsewhere. No point in re-inventing the wheel.

By using these methods we could get the numbers of tests down to a manageable level, and minimise animal testing.

More generally, we must stop the EU coming up with new legislative proposals, without properly looking at the costs to the economy (and in this case, to animals). In the USA, they have an excellent system of Regulatory Impact Assessment, and they throw out proposals likely to do more damage than they are worth. In the EU, we have nominal Economic Impact Statements, but these are usually cursory and formulaic in the extreme. Conservative MEPs will continue to argue for effective regulatory impact assessment of EU legislative proposals. ᛋᛒᛋ

And the next piece. also form November 2001, was my petulant response to the e-mail assault by the pro-vitamin lobby, which almost brought the European parliament's computer system to its knees!

Vitamins Yes — e-mail Lobbying No!

As a Euro-MP, I am constantly lobbied on a whole range of issues, from animal welfare to the Afghan war. And I am delighted to get the views of East Midlands voters. The number of letters reflects to some extent the importance that the electorate attaches to the issue.

But it can get out of hand. I (and my colleagues) have had literally thousands of e-mails on the CODEX ALIMENTARIUS (and another one pops up on my computer screen as I type these words). The Codex sounds as though it might be something to do with mediæval witchcraft, or perhaps an obscure Latin cook-book. In fact, it's a new European regulatory proposal on vitamins.

The huge volume of e-mails is clogging up the parliament's system (which was never very fast to start with). It is taking minutes to open a single e-mail, and ages to delete one. A further problem is that it is impossible to tell where an e-mail comes from. I always try to reply to communications from East Midlands electors. But these might come from anywhere — many are obviously from continental Europe or even America — so I'm afraid they get deleted without reply. If you've sent one and got no response I apologise — but you understand the problem! If you try again, add the words "From the East Midlands" in the first line, and I'll get back to you.

So what's the problem with vitamins? Well the EU has a lunatic passion for regulating and harmonising everything, so they want to harmonise the size of vitamin tablets. Trouble is, they've got confused about the so-called "RDA" (recommended daily allowance) figures. These were invented during the second world war as a bare minimum to prevent deficiency diseases. But the EU, in effect, wants to make them maximums.

For example, you need 50 mgs of Vitamin C (the RDA), to prevent scurvy. But many people, me included, like to take much higher doses when we feel down, or have a cold. 1000 mgs is not uncommon. So under the original EU proposals, you'd have to take twenty tablets (of 50 mgs) to get what many people consider a reasonable dose. Similar figures apply to other vitamins.

In fact we seem to have seen off mandatory limits, but the mere fact of the proposal illustrates the need for constant vigilance.

These low limits are used in Germany. And the EU, applying the so-called "precautionary principle", wants to take the German rules and apply them to us all. There is a theory (expressed in many of the e-mails) that it is all a wicked plot by the drug companies to deny us healthy vitamins and force us to get sick and use prescription medicines. I doubt that. I think it's just the EU's familiar obsession with regulation, with the Nanny State, with telling us what we can and can't do.

Many of the e-mails contain heart-rending stories of sick people who depend on high-dose vitamins to keep going. They are pleading with us not to ban them.

I agree. I think the EU's proposals are daft. I shall vote against them. I should still have voted against them if I'd never received a single e-mail.

But I'm tearing my hair out at the tidal wave of junk e-mails. If there's one thing that could change my mind and get me to support the European Commission's position on this one, it would be the assault by the e-mail lobbyists! *ƽↄƽↄƽↄ*

> *Sir Eddie George, Governor of the Bank of England:*
> *"Britain joining the Euro would be like an elephant getting into a rowing boat".*

Chapter Eleven

The Human Rights Agenda

The EU produces proposals with wonderful, motherhood-and-apple-pie titles that seem impossible to vote against. Yet the contents and the effects of the proposals may be very dangerous indeed. Nowhere is this truer than in the field of "human rights" proposals. This first piece is from November 2000.

Freedom Under Fire

The so-called Charter of Fundamental Rights is one of the most dangerous, illiberal and anti-democratic measures ever to come out of the EU. Let me tell you why.

Any sensible institution would decide first what a document was for, then write it. The EU has adopted the opposite approach with the Charter. It had a committee write it without knowing whether it was to be included in the Treaty of Nice, and thus become law, or whether it was to be a mere declaration. Tony Blair insists that it will be merely declaratory, though many continental leaders want it in the Treaty. Let's hope that for once Mr. Blair will use his veto.

But there is a perverse logic to the EU's approach. EU leaders and lawyers have already said that even if the Charter is a mere declaration, the courts will "take it into account". In other words, it becomes European law in effect whether we agree to it or not.

Democracy has shallow roots on the continent. Most continental countries have had right-wing dictatorship in my lifetime. Perhaps they need written constitutions. But in Britain, by contrast, our rights derive from the long centuries in which our democracy has developed, and from the slow evolution of our common law. We don't need politicians or governments or institutions to give us our rights. We were born with them. They are our inalienable birthright.

I recently had dinner with Margaret Thatcher. One of my colleagues asked for her view on the Charter. She fixed him with her magisterial stare, and said "Young man, you cannot legislate for fundamental rights. In this country we have democracy, and that is good enough". Spot on, as always.

The Charter, therefore, offers us nothing new. But in Clause 52, it threatens to take away the rights we already have. It says that the EU can suspend our rights "in the interests of the Union". In other words, on an official's whim. This is what constitutional lawyers call *raison d'etat* - reasons of state. Hitler's Nazi constitution for Germany contained just such a clause, allowing the constitution to be suspended "in the national interest" - in other words, whenever Hitler fancied it.

The Charter is thus a monstrous threat to our historic liberties.

We have seen this week how our rights may be attacked by Europe. The Advocate General of the European Court of Justice (ECJ) has said that criticism of the European Union goes beyond fair political comment, and is "akin to blasphemy". It could thus be suppressed without prejudice to freedom of speech! This caused huge embarrassment, and the European Institutions tried desperately to deny the facts - even quoting a wrong case number on the court's website.

In the European parliament they really do take criticism of the European project almost as blasphemy. They regard those who believe in the nation state as most Brits do, as if we were wild men from the mountains, coming into the parliament in loincloths and woad. I have been asked how I, with my opinions, qualify as an MEP. What right do I have to be there? I reply that I was elected not to build the European dream, but to represent the voters of the East Midlands. My right to be there is that I was elected number one on the East Midlands list, fair and square with no recounts.

If the judges and lawyers and *apparatchiks* of the ECJ really want a test case of their doctrine that criticism of the EU amounts to blasphemy, then I have a message for them. I'm first in line. They'll find plenty of evidence in my book and in my articles for regional newspapers. C'mon guys. Make my day!
ᔕᔕᔕᔕ

Prompted by Home Secretary David Blunkett's embarrassment — and obvious anger — at the effects of the European Convention of Human Rights, I returned to the subject in October 2001.

Human Rights and Wrongs

Some East Midlands voters seem to think that Euro-MPs are entirely useless. Others think we have unlimited powers. Indeed, one or two who have written to me appear to hold both these views at the same time.

I am constantly hearing from constituents with a problem or grievance — perhaps they need a zebra crossing, or they are opposed to a rubbish tip, or they're having problems with a planning authority — who are convinced that theirs is a human rights issue, and ask me if I will "Take it to the European Court".

Of course I can't do that, for a whole range of reasons. First of all, Euro-MPs make laws — they don't plead cases in court. If you want to bring a court case, you need a lawyer. Secondly, the European Court of Human Rights in Strasbourg is actually not part of the EU institutions (although the European Court of Justice in Luxembourg is — confusing, isn't it?). It was set up by the Council of Europe, which includes 42 European countries — most not EU members.

Our current Labour government has incorporated the European Convention on Human Rights into British law, so you can now bring a human rights case in your local British court — no need to go to Strasbourg. But rather than risk the costs of a court case, you may do better to talk to the Citizens' Advice Bureau, your local Council or your Westminster MP.

Bringing the Convention into British law was a flagship policy of Labour's 1997 manifesto, and it has blown up spectacularly in their faces. It is deeply ironic to hear Home Secretary David Blunkett complaining about the judges who have given unexpected rulings based on the Convention. Blunkett was shocked when four asylum seekers recently won a case for wrongful detention (even though it was overturned on appeal). It seems that Labour's proposals for punishing anthrax hoaxers may fall foul of the Convention.

A whole range of sensible measures to deal with asylum seekers or terrorist suspects are outlawed by the Convention. It is incredible, but true, that if Osama bin Laden were to be arrested in Leicester, we actually wouldn't be able to extradite him to the USA!

This illustrates the danger of high-flown "Conventions" and "Charters" of rights. They sound marvellous — how on earth can you oppose them, I am asked. Yet they allow unelected and unaccountable judges to build a structure of case-law that often flies in the face of common sense.

You may not like what politicians do, and what they decide, but at least you can vote the rascals out at the next election. The effect of these broad, loosely worded Charters of Rights is to pass decision-making from sackable politicians to unsackable judges. We may all live to regret it. ❧❧❧

Following the terrorist outrages of September 11th 2001, proposals have been brought forward for a European Arrest Warrant.

The European Arrest Warrant

Following the atrocities of September 11th, there has been a flurry of activity aimed at tightening security and bearing down on terrorists. Home Secretary David Blunkett has introduced a range of proposals, and is facing criticism, not least from his own back-benchers, that his plans are a threat to civil liberties.

The EU has used the terrorists' attacks in a wholly cynical and opportunist way to progress proposals for a "Single European Area of Justice". These are plans that they have been developing for years, but which have been rightly resisted by member states as an excessive invasion of national sovereignty. Now, the global emergency as given Brussels a window of opportunity.

The key proposal here is the "European Arrest Warrant". Contrary to what some politicians have said, this is not simply a case of "streamlining extradition". If it were, and proper safeguards were observed, no-one could object to it.

What it means is simply this — that we abandon the due process of extradition entirely, and that for a specified range of offences, it would be enough for a magistrate in Portugal or Greece to issue an arrest warrant, and that the British police would then implement that warrant, and arrest a British subject and send him abroad without any recourse to British courts.

A couple of years ago I used to warn audiences that unless we put a stop to the EU's plans for *"Corpus Juris",* the day would come when we could be arrested on the streets of our home town and sent abroad to face foreign justice with no right of appeal. I think my listeners thought that even if I had not quite taken leave of my senses, I was, perhaps, scare-mongering. Not a bit of it. It is happening now.

As I write, there are a dozen innocent British plane-spotters in a Greek jail, awaiting trial on spying charges. It seems that the Greeks have never heard of plane-spotting, and cannot believe that even the Brits would engage in such a lunatic activity. Therefore, they must be spies, even though they are nationals of another EU member-state, and of a member of NATO.

If these are the standards of justice and common sense we can expect in Greece, how can we accept a common arrest warrant? Surely one of the fundamental duties of a nation-state is to protect its citizens through its own legal system, and not hand them over without appeal or due process to foreign courts?

It is proposed that the warrant could apply to actions which are offences in the issuing country but not in the respondent's country. For example, Germany has an offence of "Holocaust denial", which we in Britain do not have. Now I regard Holocaust denial as both stupid and objectionable. But free speech demands that we be allowed to say our piece, even if it is stupid and objectionable. The idea that we could be arrested on a German warrant and sent off to face trial abroad is surely more objectionable still.

They want to include racism and xenophobia in the list of qualifying offences. Now all decent people oppose racism and xenophobia, but with political correctness running riot, who knows what innocent opinion may not be caught in the net? And it is a commonplace in the EU institutions for closet federalists to apply the word "xenophobe" to anyone who opposes further European integration, or who — horror of horrors — wants to wind back the ratchet of integration.

Turncoat MEP Bill Newton Dunn has actually described me as a xenophobe (I responded by sending him a dictionary, as he seemed confused about the meaning of words).

A majority of the British people oppose joining the Euro. Is it too far-fetched to imagine that opposing Euro membership might become an arrestable offence under these proposals? ꝫꝭꝫꝭ

At an Environment Committee meeting on January 26th 2000, Irish MEP and Senator Avril Doyle drew attention to a colony of rare snails which had caused the re-routing of a by-pass around the city of Kildare. Within minutes, East Midlands Labour MEP Phillip Whitehead had circulated the following:

A snail that once lived in Kildare
Was accustomed to taking the air
It refused its permission
To the EU Commision
For a road which would tarmac its lair

Chapter Twelve

The Treaty of Nice

Anyone who doubts the direction, and the ratchet effect, of the European project, has only to look at the inexorable, unstoppable sequence of treaties. The Treaty of Rome. The Single European Act. The Maastricht Treaty. The Amsterdam Treaty. And now the Treaty of Nice, agreed but not yet ratified. Even that is not the end. A further treaty is envisaged for 2004. And the objective of that treaty is nothing less than a European constitution.

In June 2000 I anticipated the up-coming Treaty of Nice.

Not a NICE Treaty At All

Feisty Caroline Jackson, Tory MEP for the South West and Chairman of the European parliament's Environment Committee, has a school-mistressly manner coupled with a wicked, dry sense of humour. At a recent committee meeting, when weary MEPs were having trouble lifting their arms after voting on a couple of hundred amendments, she chided us: "Come along now. Get on with it. At least this is better than shooting at each other on the Western Front".

Of course she had broken the Parliament's unwritten rule – *Don't mention the War!* William Hague was careful not to mention the war when he recently said "European integration represents the greatest threat to British sovereignty and independence for fifty years". But clearly he had the war in mind.

We now face the latest and most vicious turn of the screw – the current Intergovernmental Conference, or IGC. This is expected to lead to a Treaty of Nice, under the French presidency, to be agreed in December 2000, although it will then need to be ratified at Westminster (of which more later). It will stand in a long and infamous tradition – the Treaty of Rome, the Single European Act, Maastricht, Amsterdam. Each has represented a new milestone on the road to a federal super-state. Nice may be one of the last milestones, because we are nearly there already.

As usual, the Euro-quislings are playing it down. It will just pick up a few left-overs from Amsterdam. Just some tidying-up of the institutions to make way for enlargement. Clearly we will need changes in numbers of Commissioners and MEPs, for example, before the EU grows to comprise twenty-five members. If only that were all.

In a sense, we cannot say what will be in the Treaty until it is signed in December. But the Commission and the Parliament have already put forward their views. The Parliament's document was described by the Daily Telegraph as "One of the most federalist documents ever to come out of a European institution". To his eternal shame, one of my Conservative MEP colleagues actually voted **for** it (I and 32 others voted against).

So, a flavour of what to expect. They want to eliminate the veto on all decisions but treaty changes (and there are even proposals to allow the Commission itself to change the treaties in some circumstances). In particular, there is a huge head of steam behind the idea of majority voting on taxation and economic management. We see here the incremental nature of our long defeat. First the Europhiles said that there was no question of tax harmonisation. Then, well of course the EU could have a say on VAT – wasn't this part of their remit, and their funding base? And it was reasonable to ask for a withholding tax, wasn't it, to prevent evasion? Then perhaps common bands for corporate taxes to avoid "unfair tax competition"? But surely no EU say on personal taxes, at least? Give them time, give them time!

They want EU-wide political parties, with state funding. Prompted by the Freedom Party's success in Austria, there are proposals for EU sanctions against parties that don't adopt "European values". This is really sinister. In the old Eastern Europe, they never banned elections. They just banned any political party that disagreed with the state. This is the thin end of a potentially totalitarian wedge. It wouldn't take too much imagination to decide that the Tory party had failed to adopt sufficiently European attitudes.

Then there are proposals to expand EuroPol and establish a European Public Prosecutor. Initially this would be for "crimes against the EU" (why does that, too, send a shiver up my spine?), but with *corpus juris* in the background, we all know where the salami tactics will lead us. How long before an Englishman is arrested in Market Harborough by a Greek policeman who speaks no English?

They say they want flexibility in the Treaty. But don't be deceived. This is one of those weasel words (like subsidiarity or federalism) which means different things to different people. Personally I fully support flexibility, by which I mean that, beyond the core rights and responsibilities of the Single Market (interpreted narrowly), member states should be able to pick'n'mix other EU policies, on a menu-driven basis. But the give-away is the alternative term they use – flexibility or **enhanced co-operation**! In other words, in EU-speak flexibility means no more than a right to integrate faster, with the assumption that all member states will eventually catch up.

Then we come to the so-called Charter of Fundamental Rights. This was dreamed up on a dull afternoon at a Heads-of-Government Summit at Helsinki last December, apparently with the sole objective of "bringing Europe closer to the people" – in other words, a publicity stunt to persuade Europeans that the EU project actually delivers something worthwhile. But like so many European ideas, it has taken on a life of its own, driven by the hyper-active institutions.

The key question is whether this charter will stand alone as a mere aspirational declaration, or whether it will be incorporated into the Treaty of Nice. Both Labour and the Tory party agree that if we must have it, it should be a declaration without the force of law, but it seems inevitable that it will become part of the Treaty, and therefore justiciable before the European Court of Justice (ECJ). Given Tony Blair's passion to strut the European stage, and his manifest embarrassment at his failure to con the British people into the Euro, he is likely to give way on this one. It is critical that the Tory Party should not only oppose it, but commit itself to repealing it if enacted.

The Charter is offensive for two reasons. First of all, for its contents. Secondly, because of its legal and constitutional implications.

Human rights are already well catered for, so this Charter will include "social rights". This could include a right to work. It could include a range of trade union rights that would roll back the reforms of the Thatcher years and lock us into the failed European Social model.

Worse than that, the Charter brings huge new policy areas under European competence. For example, imagined slights in education or health could result in actions before the ECJ. The ECJ will treat the Charter not as a completed body of law, but as a foundation on which they can build a massive new super-structure of interpretation and precedent. The ECJ is mostly socialist and passionately federalist, and the last thing we want is to give them the opportunity to create more judge-made law, entirely free of democratic oversight.

It would, in effect, be a constitution for a European state. At a meeting in Brussels on June 7th, Angela Merkel, the new leader of the German CDU (and possibly the next Chancellor of Germany), said "The Charter should be in the Treaty. We could call it a constitutional Treaty. It would be a new constitution for a United States of Europe". The cat is out of the bag. Don't say they didn't tell us.

Both the Charter and the Treaty are thoroughly bad things. We should be looking at ways to dismantle the EU's oppressive and outdated institutions and competences, and returning powers to the nation state. The great task of our time is European deconstruction. These new plans go in exactly the wrong direction. We should re-establish Britain as an independent nation, trading globally. Of course we want to co-operate and trade with Europe, but we also want to develop competitiveness and prosperity free of Euro-regulation, and we want close relations with the more dynamic markets of the USA and Asia.

Britain cannot go on as it is in Europe. The balance of advantage is accelerating into negative territory. The recent IOD report showed that the net cost of membership, after factoring in the undoubted trade advantages, was between £15 and £25 billion. This could double with tax harmonisation.

It is not Tory policy to withdraw from the EU. But if we are to stay in, we must renegotiate our terms so that at least from our point of view, the EU looks and behaves like a free trade area, nothing more. And we must accept, as a fall-back position, that if it proves impossible to achieve this result after a sincere and genuine attempt at re-negotiation, then the withdrawal question must be re-opened. We will have membership on our terms, or not at all.
ৼৼৼ

Blair came back from the Nice negotiations full of spin and self-congratulation, rather as John Major did from Maastricht, with his "Game, set and match to Britain". The years have taken the gloss off Major's achievement at Maastricht, but it took only weeks for the gilt to come off Mr. Blair's gingerbread.

Did Blair Win at Nice?

Now that the dust has settled on the EU's Nice summit, it's time for a cool look at the outcome. Tony Blair came home trumpeting his "success" in keeping the tax veto. But of course all he had to do was say No. And he gave away Britain's national veto in dozens of other areas.

But Blair's success on the tax veto won't last. The EU has a whole raft of new tax harmonisation measures in the pipeline. They propose transport taxes on road charges, parking, rail and station use, air travel and motor insurance. Labour's MEPs support these proposals — and Labour Commissioner Neil Kinnock invented them! Last month in Strasbourg Labour MEPs supported proposals to extend VAT to digital services, and to tax aviation fuel. They even demanded full-scale harmonisation of VAT, which would end the UK's zero-rate opt-outs. This could put Euro-VAT on food and children's clothes — and even on Granny's funeral.

It was as early as December 1997 that Labour signed up to the EU's tax proposals, at the Ecofin meeting, with a code of conduct in business taxation. And the working group on so-called "unfair tax competition" (Euro-speak for competitive tax rates) is chaired by none other than Red Dawn Primorolo, Tony Blair's own Labour Treasury Minister. Their new Code of Conduct so far covers only corporate tax, but the group's remit is on-going. The EU has conspicuously failed to guarantee that the group's mandate won't be extended to personal tax.

A low tax environment is a magnet for business and inward investment. This is proved by the experience of Ireland, where low corporate tax rates have helped drive rapid growth. But of course high-tax countries resent the success of low-tax countries. The EU's tax harmonisation proposals would hurt not only businesses and shareholders, but workers and pensioners as well. High tax means low growth, low investment and high unemployment.

Of course there is really no such thing as "harmful tax competition". Harmonised taxes are a cartel operated by governments against the people. All tax competition is good. We need more, not less of it. The Irish example shows how low tax rates can transform an economy delivering significant improvements in living standards for ordinary people.

Europe has a choice between the Anglo-Saxon model based on tax competition, or the EU's corporatist cartel-model which uses harmonisation to protect the tax base from competition.

The EU Commission is convinced that it has won this fight. It has instituted a full-scale study of business tax in the EU, and is confident it can rail-road through its ideas.

Did Tony Blair win in Nice? No. He got a couple of good headlines, but the process of integration goes on. British prosperity and independence are still under threat. We need a government in Westminster that will face up to that threat, and put British interests first. ᶻ♥ᶻ♥ᶻ♥

The above article is a resumé of a longer piece by Theresa Villiers, a London Tory MEP who sits on the European Parliament's Monetary Policy Committee

Note: The Nice Treaty received its third reading in the House of Commons in October 2001. But of course it was rejected by Ireland, and cannot take legal effect until ratified by all 15 member states.

One of the projects driven forward by the Nice Treaty was the European Army. Another was the increase in voting weight proposed for Germany — breaking, for the first time in EU history, the long-standing parity between France and Germany. In May 2001, I leapt to the defence of one of our East Midlands Conservative MPs who had been criticised for warning of the increasing influence of Germany in the EU.

13 May 2001

The Editor,
The Daily Telegraph.

Dear Sir,

On Friday, my colleague Sir Peter Tapsell MP (for Louth & Horncastle) was vilified for expressing concerns about German ambitions in the EU. The next day we hear that British troops attached to the EU army will be commanded from Hermann Goering's WWII Nazi bunker.

It is a commonplace of discussion in Brussels that one of France's key objectives in the EU is to bind Germany into a democratic Europe and so lay to rest the ghost of German nationalism. Why is it OK for Eurocrats in Brussels to worry about German ambitions, but not for a Tory MP in the East Midlands?

Yesterday, I addressed a Euro-critical conference in Warsaw, Poland. It is clear that many Poles share Sir Peter's concerns. One man's eastward perspective is another man's *"Lebensraum"*.

Yours sincerely,

ROGER HELMER MEP

Chapter Thirteen

Education

As a Euro-MP, I naturally write rather a lot about European issues. But occasionally a domestic issue comes to the fore. This article dates from July 2001.

Spare the Rod – Spoil the Child

Two stories on this morning's BBC news struck me.

First story: six Canadian children were dragged kicking and screaming from their parents by police and social workers and taken to a "place of safety". Why? Because the parents believed in moderate physical punishment as part of a wholesome discipline.

Second story: two South African teachers, who had worked in Hackney for a year, were going home to warn other teachers against coming to Britain. Why? Because the indiscipline, insolence, and foul-mouthed abuse from the Hackney children was worse, they said, than they would expect from the most deprived township in South Africa.

Is it just possible that poor discipline in schools is something to do with the fact that teachers have no credible sanctions anymore? I remember a dreadful secret camera programme from a comprehensive school, broadcast a couple of years back. Whenever the teacher tried to remonstrate with a pupil, she was met with an insolent "What yer gonna do about it, then?". That is the teachers' problem, because there is nothing they can do about it, and the kids know it.

We read of a lesbian teacher who has been driven out of her job by constant verbal abuse, in and out of school. Now I personally think she was very unwise to parade her minority sexual orientation in front of the pupils, but I am horrified at the total breakdown of order that allows a teacher to be hounded out of her job by constant insults and abuse.

We read of teachers persecuted through the courts, sometimes on the uncorroborated word of a single child, accused of assault. Even if the alleged incident took place at all, it was frequently something that most sensible people would feel was quite justified in the circumstances. One teacher's career was ruined when she was accused of "prodding a boy in the chest" with her finger.

Is it any wonder that recent research shows that most teachers don't expect to be in the profession in five year's time, or that a third of them are considering applying for jobs in the independent sector, where discipline is better?

We now have a generation of parents who themselves have no experience of an orderly school, and sadly a few of them when presented with a disciplinary problem are as likely to assault the teacher as to control the child.

Yet throughout recorded history, and still in most areas of the world, moderate physical discipline of children is considered not only permissible, but essential and entirely proper. In Singapore, which I have visited over thirty years (and where I had the privilege of living in during 1994), they retain the cane for offences like street crime and vandalism. Young tearaways who get the cane in Singapore are unlikely to sit down for a month. They are also very unlikely to re-offend. This is why Singapore is one of the safest cities in the world.

Of course the politically correct Moaning Minnies and bleeding-hearts will say that physical punishment only teaches children that violence is the solution. Stuff and nonsense. It is the breakdown of decent standards, it is violence and intimidation and bullying in the playground that teach children to resort to violence. By contrast, a decent, safe, orderly and respectful school environment, with corporal punishment as a rarely-used but available sanction, teaches self-discipline and control.

And it is an orderly environment that enables education to take place. So which is the kindest option? To give a child a good, orderly education which will prepare them for life, with an outside chance of the cane for serious misbehaviour? Or to send them to a school where order has broken down, where the law of the jungle applies in the playground and sometimes in the classroom, where the teachers are depressed and desperate to leave, where all they will learn is bullying and foul-mouthed insolence?

Discipline and order are the pre-requisites for education. Without them, no amount of changes to content or curriculum will do any good. ❧❧❧

Even a domestic issue like education can have a European angle, as this next piece from November 2001 shows.

Captain Euro Strikes Again!

All over the country, in hundreds of schools, our children are being brain-washed at the tax-payer's expense, by a torrent of Euro-propaganda. A flood of "teaching aids" — wall-charts, maps, books and brochures — starts influencing them as soon as they start their education. And it never stops.

The Eurocrats know from their own research that the idea of European integration is becoming less and less popular across the EU, but they are determined to fight back. With their catchy comic-book character "Captain Euro", they are attacking the most vulnerable target — our children. (If you think this is too bizarre to be true, and that I must be making it up, just check out their web-site www.captaineuro.com, where you'll find the new "European Super-Hero", and also meet his sworn enemy, Dr. D. Vider — geddit?).

Former Belgian EU Commissioner Willy de Clercq understood the game. He briefed his propaganda team to "act where resistance is weakest".

No-one seems to care that under the 1996 Education Act, it is specifically forbidden to use material on contentious issues that is not objective, impartial and balanced. This EU propaganda campaign is actually illegal.

They repeatedly use the word "Europe" to mean the EU, although the EU is only fifteen countries, while the Council of Europe recognises 43. And they constantly seek to suggest that nations can do nothing by themselves, that the only solutions to problems are European solutions. Their specific objective is to undermine our children's independence and identity as British subjects.

They never mention the costs of converting Britain to the Euro, which independent estimates put as high as £36 billion — about the cost of running the NHS for a year. Still less do they talk of the macro-economic damage which will result from imposing a one-size-fits-all interest rate on diverse economies. This will lead to the wrong interest rate for most countries, most of the time, causing boom and bust. They never mention the looming pensions crisis in Europe, which means that a vote for the Euro is a vote for higher taxes, higher interest rates, higher unemployment.

There is nothing about the destruction of our fisheries under the Common Fisheries Policy, or the damage to our agriculture caused by the CAP. Nothing about the way our competitiveness is undermined and enterprise stifled by the suffocating weight of Euro-regulation and the "European social model".

This systematic assault on our education system is not limited to the schools. In our universities, over 100 professorships are directly funded by the EU. These "Jean Monet" chairs are specifically intended to teach undergraduates about the EU and to promote the gospel of integration. In August 2000, Brussels launched an initiative to target the curricula. Needless to say, history and economics were high on the agenda, closely followed by politics and geography.

What can we do to counter this assault on our nation? I suggest that you write to the Chairman of Governors at your child's school, asking whether they use EU propaganda materials, and if so, what steps they take to ensure balance. (They could start with the Institute of Directors' study that shows the net cost of British membership of the EU is between £15 and £30 billion a year). And you could remind them that if they fail to ensure balance and objectivity, they are in breach of the law. ❧❧❧

Cecil Rhodes: *"The greatest prize in the lottery of life is to be born an Englishman".*

Chapter Fourteen

God Bless the Queen!

Another topic which I have had cause to write about is that of the Monarchy. We may not take Labour's closet republicans seriously, but they are dismembering most of our most respected institutions, and it would be foolish to think they won't have a go at the Monarchy next. After all, they will say, if we agreed that the hereditary principle was unacceptable for the House of Lords, how can we accept it for the House of Windsor?

This piece was prompted by the Sophie Rhys-Jones affair in April 2001.

Royalist and Proud of it

Pity the poor Royals. They take stick whatever they do. If they avoid any gainful employment other than their Royal duties, then they're parasites and wasters living off the public purse. But the moment they go out and get a proper job, the lizards of Fleet Street are spilling ink over "conflicts of interest". Sophie Rhys-Jones' PR company trades on her Royal connections, they say. Prince Edward – horror of horrors – talks business to contacts he meets on Royal visits. As if any businessman worth his salt would not seize on opportunities thrown up by chance meetings.

Sophie was certainly naïve and careless to be taken in by the fake sheikh. But is there anyone at all in business or in public life who has not at some time said something careless to the press and lived to regret it? Certainly not me. I got caught out by Channel 4's Mark Thomas Product only recently.

Sophie is new in the job; she's entitled to a few mistakes. Have we already forgotten what the media did to the last beautiful young woman who married into the Royal family? If you read what Sophie actually said, it's all pretty yawn-making stuff. As the Telegraph said, a gaffe is when a public person says out loud what everyone else privately thinks.

It's extraordinary that the Windsors have taken so much flak, when the villain of the piece is the News of the World and its odious undercover reporter Mazher Mahmood. Their behaviour was simply unforgivable. Mahmood deserves to be ostracised by all decent people for the rest of time. The European Convention of Human Rights, now enshrined in UK law, offers a right of privacy. It seems to me that there is a *prima facie* case that the News of the World has breached the Convention.

Closely following Mahmood in the blame stakes are the Labour Ministers. Stephen Byers (Bozo to his friends) is outrageously patronising. Kim Howells actually questions the future of the monarchy in Britain, and no-one from Number 10 rebukes him. Labour's closet republicans are coming out.

They say that the Royal family isn't worth the money. That's wrong on two counts. First, the government's income from the Crown Estates exceeds the Civil List. The Royal Family more than pays its way. Second, royalty and pageantry are an essential element in Britain's tourism offering. On any reasonable estimate the Royals pay for themselves over again by the foreign visitors they attract.

The republicans ask how we justify the hereditary principle. But that is precisely what keeps our head of state out of politics. If you want an elected head of state, imagine whom you might get. Would you prefer Bill Clinton or Boris Yeltsin? Or a nonentity like Germany's President Johannes Rau – who recently called for a European constitution and federation? Or perhaps you'd prefer Neil Kinnock when he's finished his stint in Brussels?

They ask what the monarchy is **for**. Well the Queen does have a key rôle in advising Prime Ministers – she's had more experience in the job than any of them. And she has a pivotal task in the event of a hung parliament, in deciding whom to call on to form a government. But above all, we need a non-political head of state, who would provide a focus and a shared identity for the whole of the United Kingdom, if only the press would call off the dogs and let her get on with it.

I was born a subject of the King, I am proud to be a subject of the Queen, and I intend to die a British subject, not a European citizen. ❧❧❧

The President of the European parliament, Nicole Fontaine (1999 to 2002) is not content to do her job as speaker of the house and shop-steward-in-chief of the MEPs. She sees herself as a sort of minor head of state and ambassador, and loves to travel the world meeting important people. A meeting she had with Her Majesty the Queen in June 2000 had some interesting consequences.

A Question of Identity

Do you identify yourself with your county? Or do you think of yourself as English? As a Brit? Or as part of some larger unit?

The question struck me last week, following an audience which the Queen gave to the President of the European Parliament, Nicole Fontaine. I suppose we must forgive the French for not understanding the normal rules of British protocol, but Mrs. Fontaine made two key errors. First of all, she didn't understand that the Queen, as a non-political head of state, never expresses personal opinions on political issues, although sometimes, when appropriate, she will simply state the position of the government of the day. Secondly, it appears that Mrs. Fontaine did not know that audiences with the Queen are privileged and confidential.

So she rushed out and gave an interview to the press, and on July 1st the Independent newspaper ran a story about the Queen's enthusiasm for Britain to join the Euro.

I raised Mrs. Fointaine's *faux pas* as a point of order in Strasbourg on Monday July 3rd. To my astonishment, a senior Labour MEP Bill Miller – he's Labour's Chief Whip in the European parliament – compounded Mrs. Fontaine's error by asking me "to congratulate the Queen on her opinion about the Euro". He did this not once, but three times, on Monday, Tuesday and Wednesday.

While Mrs. Fontaine may be forgiven for not knowing the rules that apply to audiences with the Queen, Mr. Miller has no such excuse, and his blatant attempt to drag the Queen's name into a contentious political issue was nothing short of disgraceful. So on Thursday morning I got up on a point of order and gave Mr. Miller the rough edge of my tongue. In particular, I said that although I was proud to be British, I was ashamed that day to share my nationality with Mr. Miller.

In his reply, Mr. Miller, having totally failed to answer my criticism, remarked that he was a Scot, he was British, but that "unlike Mr. Helmer, I am also European".

Here at last Mr. Miller was right. I don't feel European at all, and I reject and repudiate the concept of "European citizenship" enshrined in the Maastricht Treaty.

The American satirical writer P.J. O'Rourke has a marvellous phrase to describe what Churchill used to call "The English Speaking Peoples" – the British, Americans, Canadians, Australians and New Zealanders. O'Rourke describes them as "Very Great Britain Indeed", and perhaps surprisingly for an Irish American, he is happy to associate himself with that idea.

Unlike Mr. Miller, I see myself as an Englishman and a Brit, but also as part of "Very Great Britain Indeed" – the English Speaking Peoples, who have so much in common in terms of language, history, shared culture, and a similar approach to enterprise and society. It's a question of identity. For me, as for many Brits, the foreigners start at Calais. ৵৵৵৵

This is the point of order which I felt that I had to make in the Strasbourg plenary session on these events, so that my criticism of Bill Miller would be read into the parliamentary record.

Madame President:

On Monday, I made a point of order about your reported comments in the British press regarding your recent meeting with Her Majesty Queen Elizabeth II. A British Labour member of this house, Mr. Miller, repeated what were purported to be the Queen's remarks, not once but three times, on Monday, Tuesday and Wednesday. He sought to drag the Queen into a political controversy and use her name to score cheap political points.

Madame President, it may be that you were unfamiliar with the British rules of protocol which obtain in such matters, but Mr. Miller has no such excuse. He knows perfectly well that ours is a non-political head of state. He knows perfectly well that for nearly fifty years she has scrupulously avoided contentious political issues. He knows perfectly well that she cannot come to this house to set the record straight.

Madame President, I am proud to be British, but today I am ashamed to share my nationality with Mr. Miller. Has HE no shame? Has he no respect? Has he no decency or honour? ৵৵৵৵

Frankfurt economist Wilhelm Hankel:
"Historically, monetary unions have an average survival time
of twelve to fifteen years.
That's what I give the euro".

Chapter Fifteen

Agriculture, Energy, Transport

This is the nearest it gets to a "miscellaneous" chapter — four pieces that don't quite fit under other chapter-headings! The first piece is from September 2000.

When is a Vet not a Vet?

There's a crisis in the meat industry. Farmers, abattoirs and independent butchers could be ruined and forced to close. Your favourite high-street butcher may not be there in twelve months' time. Why? Because the enormous pressure and cost of regulation and inspection, particularly in small abattoirs, is killing them. Dozens of small abattoirs have closed in recent months.

It's perfectly possible to have four men working in a small abattoir and four other men watching them. Not popping in now and again to check, but all the time. As a constituent said to William Hague recently, "If it goes on like this, Mr. Hague, we'll have one man working in Britain and fifty million watching him".

Why do small abattoirs matter? They are the lynch-pin of the distribution system from small farmers to local butchers. Big farmers, in general, use big abattoirs and sell on to supermarkets. But big abattoirs don't want to know about a small farmer with a dozen beasts – nor do they want to sell small quantities to high-street butchers.

Take away the small abattoirs, and the farmers and butchers both suffer.

There's also a very strong animal welfare case for small, local abattoirs. It is much less stressful for an animal to go to a local slaughterhouse than to be trucked a hundred miles to a big abattoir. Short journeys mean better quality meat as well.

Why are the costs of regulation and inspection being pushed out of sight? There is a whole range of reasons. Special measures because of BSE. The general European habit of creating tons of paperwork. The tendency of our own civil servants in Whitehall to "Gold Plate" European legislation – drafting it much more tightly than they need to, and much more tightly than other member states.

But one key problem seems to be simply a matter of translation, years ago. It came to my attention when I was invited to speak recently at the national convention of the Association of Meat Inspectors at the Harper Adams Agricultural College in Shropshire. Early EU directives called for veterinarians to inspect abattoirs, to provide certificates and so on.

It is not at all clear that the original intention was to require fully qualified vets – veterinary surgeons – to inspect and oversee slaughterhouses. After all, vets are trained to cure gerbils and set broken legs in dogs – skills rarely required in the average abattoir. Meantime Meat Inspectors are highly qualified people in the specific issues that matter in the meat trade. The vets who are required by law to stand and watch in slaughterhouses may well be over-qualified, and may – dare I say – be merely duplicating the work that can be done perfectly well by meat inspectors.

Could we be doubling-up inspections, driving up the cost of meat, making our British agriculture less competitive, closing local abattoirs and independent butchers, just because of a simple misinterpretation of the intent of the legislation? Surely we couldn't have been so daft as that? I'm afraid we could. Certainly the meat inspectors think so. After a year in the European parliament, I have learned never to underestimate the depths of folly to which the European project can sink.

The Tory party is dedicated to cutting red tape and bureaucratic nonsense. Of course all parties say that in opposition, then fail to deliver in government. But this time I believe we've really got the message and are prepared to be absolutely savage with the tide of regulation. The burdens on our agriculture and our abattoirs must be top of the list. ❧❧❧

In February 2001 the disaster of foot and mouth disease hit British agriculture. This comment came from March 2001.

Foot & Mouth & Europe

The current Foot and Mouth outbreak is a huge national disaster. It is a dreadful blow to farmers, who were already on their knees, but it has also hit the tourist industry, specialist hauliers, and a broad swathe of other rural businesses.

We may be tempted to look around for someone to blame. But surely even the most Eurosceptic of us could not blame the EU, could we? Well, maybe. The EU may not be the primary cause of the outbreak, but it has contributed. For a start, by driving up the cost of food in the EU, the

Common Agricultural Policy (CAP) has increased the pressure for imports, often from countries where FMD is endemic, like Argentina and Botswana.

Secondly, because trade policy is determined centrally in the EU, it is more difficult for individual member states to impose import bans on third countries when risk is suspected.

Thirdly, the imposition of draconian regulation and inspection régimes has forced the closure of huge numbers of smaller abattoirs. At a remaining small abattoir near my home in Leicestershire they typically have four people working and four people watching – no wonder they're going out of business! So animals are trucked over longer distances to larger abattoirs, which is bad for animal welfare, bad for meat quality, and increases the risk of disease transmission.

This is a classic example of the law of unintended consequences. The measures were imposed with the best will in the world, to protect the public and maintain high standards of food hygiene. But the unintended effect is the more rapid transmission of disease.

Fourthly, EU rules have delayed the disposal of slaughtered animals, which in many cases have been left lying in fields and farmyards for days, until they are bloated and stinking. Apart from the absolute horror for the farmer as he waits surrounded by carrion for the carcasses to be removed, they are a further source of contamination as birds, foxes and rats are attracted to them.

We are seeing delays in getting the vet to the farm, delays in getting tests done to confirm the disease, delays in getting the beasts slaughtered and delays in disposal. We are also – incredibly – trucking dead animals through areas which are so far disease-free, to a rendering plant in Cheshire. MAFF says it is safe to ship the carcasses. Farmers say they have seen animals' legs sticking out from under the tarpaulins.

In the 1967 outbreak, the vet came immediately, armed with a pistol; he didn't wait for tests but slaughtered suspect animals on the spot; and around 80% of the carcasses were buried within twenty-four hours.

Why are we reluctant to bury today? Because of EU environmental rules on landfill! Those regulations may be fine for normal times, but are wholly inappropriate in this national emergency.

We in the Tory party say we should make more vets available – bring back retired vets on an emergency basis, use final year vet students if necessary. Slaughter on suspicion, don't wait for tests. And dispose of the carcasses immediately. We say army should have been brought in earlier, not weeks after the first outbreak when 350 cases had been reported. And we are calling for a business-rates-holiday for rural businesses affected by the disaster.

Tony Blair was recently reported as saying that the CAP had been a disaster for consumers and for the environment, and had not done much for farmers. Congratulations to Tony for finally noticing the obvious! But his solution is to reform it. I have news for Tony. We have been trying to reform it for twenty-five years, but all we have done is to fiddle at the margin. The CAP is beyond reform. Like a sheep with FMD, it deserves to be put out of its misery. That is why we in the Tory party say we should take back national control over fisheries and agriculture from the EU. ❧❧❧

As an MEP, I am running up a substantial mileage — close to thirty thousand miles a year. So traffic congestion is an issue close to my heart.

Beating the Traffic Jams

Last Friday, I went to an exhibition on "North/South movement in the M1 Corridor in the East Midlands", at Mansfield Library. It was organised by a couple of the planning consultancies working on transport problems on the M1, and they're seeking reactions from the public.

There's a real problem on the M1 between junctions 22 and 25, as I know to my cost. If I plan to attend a function in North Notts or Derbyshire on a Friday evening, I have to find a route avoiding the motorway, or sit in jams for what seems like hours.

But it's a much bigger problem than one MEP's delayed journey. Thousands of trucks sitting idling on the M1 means more pollution and global warming. It means higher costs for delivery, and therefore higher costs for goods in the shops. And it means the East Midlands is a less attractive place to invest in than if it had better access. So it costs all of us, whether we use the motorway or not.

The consultants offered a series of ideas for improvement. More spending on motorways, or on trunk roads. Motorway tolls. Better planning. Better public transport. Public education.

But they're none too keen on motorways. Get this, from their leaflet: "More capacity tends to attract more traffic, making congestion worse". As I said to them, if that's true, then **less** capacity should mean **less** congestion, so we could solve the problem by closing lanes on the M1! It's a wonderful idea. Perhaps we could shorten NHS queues by closing wards, or reduce class sizes by firing teachers.

Of course politically correct eco-warriors love the idea that more capacity simply means more congestion, but common sense says it can't be true. In any case, do we want the government saying, in effect, "We know you want to make a journey, but we're going to cut the capacity of the motorway system to stop you doing so"? In the end, isn't the job of government to deliver services people want?

Then there is the question of road tolls. Conservatives instinctively sympathise with market-led solutions. But hang on a minute. We already pay over the odds for our roads, with the highest petrol taxes in Europe. And the cost of collection of tolls is enormously inefficient — so we shouldn't accept the EU's current plans for general infrastructure charging. I could see that there may be — just maybe — a case for tolls on highly over-subscribed routes, such as city centres, but not for motorways generally.

I believe that the solution must come from a combination of measures. A sensible level of investment in motorways and trunk roads. Promotion of better and more convenient public transport. Better Park'n'Ride schemes. And sensible planning — using brown-field sites in city centres so people can live close to their work, or putting new housing close to the new tram or metro systems that are under consideration in key East Midlands cities.

The solution, in a free country, is certainly not just to stop people travelling through congestion or excessive charges. ❧❧❧

I sit on the European parliament's committee on industry — which includes not only research and foreign trade, but also energy. I never cease to be surprised at the European institutions' instinctive prejudice against nuclear power.

Don't Let the Lights Go Out!

The Independent likes to see itself as a campaigning newspaper, but those on the sharp end of its attacks may think it runs more witch-hunts than campaigns. I should know, because it has the Tory party in its firing line.

A while ago I was helping to set up a cross-party, trans-national group in the European parliament (EP) of MEPs who share the Conservative vision of a flexible Europe of nation states. Getting wind of this story, the Independent ran a headline "Now MEPs round on Hague". Not just misleading, but the direct opposite of the truth – we were supporting Hague's policy!

During the Euro-election campaign in 1999, the paper accused me and other colleagues of "signing a secret pledge" to do various dreadful things. But I never signed any pledge. I never discussed or considered signing a pledge. Indeed I had never heard of it till I saw it in the paper. It was all a figment of journalists' over-heated imagination. They now know it to be false, because I wrote and told them so. Yet they have repeated it several times since.

The nuclear industry, and especially the Sellafield reprocessing plant, is another target for the Independent. They ran banner headlines about safety scares after the data falsification problem last year. Of course the data falsification was indefensible, and those who were responsible have paid the ultimate price – they have been sacked. But it never was a safety issue. If anything, it was a quality assurance issue, and a pretty minor one at that.

The Independent ran another safety scare story about a leak. But any major process industry will have leaks, and will have a fail-safe design to contain them. It wasn't safety. It wasn't even news. It was just routine maintenance. But the paper used it for an unjustified attack.

More recently, they ran a headline "EU to prosecute Sellafield". It was just plain wrong. The EU has no plans to prosecute Sellafield. It is outrageous that papers like the Independent can give banner headlines to false reports, and the only penalty they face is to publish a small retraction days later on an inside page. But by then the damage is done.

Of course the nuclear industry tends to get a bad press. We think of it rather as superstitious mediæval peasants regarded black magic, and many of my colleagues in the Environment Committee of the EP get the vapours when nuclear power is mentioned. So I was glad to have the opportunity to visit Sellafield last Friday and to hear their side of the case.

It came as a bit of a surprise. Did you know that Sellafield's safety record is in the top ten percent of major process industry plants in the UK? That employees' radiation exposure is less than a quarter of natural background radiation in Cornwall? And less than that of airline flight staff?

There are Irish politicians who make a living out of attacking Sellafield's tiny residual effluent into the Irish Sea, so I was surprised to learn that Irish industry puts more radiation into the Irish Sea than Sellafield does. Most major industries produce trace amounts of radioactive material. A chemical plant nearby on the West Cumbria coast also produces more radioactivity than Sellafield.

We live in a world where energy consumption is set to double in twenty-five years. Even if developed nations meet their Kyoto targets, developing countries like China and India will use vastly more energy as their economies grow. Alternative energy (wind, solar and so on), will only contribute around five percent at best. So we have only three choices.

First, we could dump nuclear and concentrate on fossil fuels, coal, gas and oil, till they run out. Global warming will speed up from a canter to a gallop. Ice-caps will melt. Sea level will rise. Bangladesh, Venice and London will be under water. France will be a desert. There will be massive migrations of refugees from the intolerable heat of the tropics – a global disaster.

Second, we can rely on nuclear energy to bridge the gap. Of course there are cost and safety implications, but these are manageable. People who challenge the economics of nuclear energy forget that coal-fired power stations get rid of their effluent free up the chimney. Cost-in that environmental damage, and nuclear looks much more attractive.

Or thirdly, we could let the lights go out.

None of these three scenarios is particularly attractive, but it seems to me that the nuclear option is a whole lot better than the others. ❧❧❧

European Riddle:

Q. How does the EU ensure the creation of new small and medium size enterprises?

A. By over-regulating large ones.

Chapter sixteen

An MEP's Life

*Every so often, someone says to me, "Yes, but what do you actually **do?**" I tried to answer the question in September 2000.*

A Day in the Life of…

Usually when people ask me "What does an MEP **do**?", I bat on about damage limitation and trying to stem the flood of badly flawed European legislation.

That's all very well, some people say, but how do you actually spend your time from hour to hour? Well yesterday was a typical Strasbourg Tuesday. The previous day I'd spent around seven hours travelling, reaching Strasbourg at lunchtime. Yesterday, I got into the office around 7:45 a.m. (checking on the way in that the Union Jack was the right way up) and spent an hour writing speeches for later on and getting a couple of letters done. BBC Radio Nottingham called for my comments on the Tory pre-manifesto document. Actually it wasn't due to be published until mid.-morning, but enough had been trailed on European policies for me to make sensible comments.

At nine, I went down to the "hemi-cycle" for the plenary session for half an hour to get the flavour of the day, before returning to my office, where I spent some time working with my research assistant on a rather technical speech for the Association of Meat Inspectors at the weekend, and getting data on EU funding for pro-Euro propaganda, for a letter which my press office was drafting to send to my constituent Keith Vaz, Minister for Europe. Bizarrely, Vaz had accused the "NO" campaign of stifling debate on the Euro — at a time when taxpayers' money is being spent on the pro campaign and the government itself is promoting the Euro!

Mid-morning, I had a long telephone chat with Sunday Telegraph journalist Christopher Booker, before going into a so-called "Solemn Session" of the parliament to hear the speaker of the Israeli Knesset and a Palestinian representative speak to MEPs. This was followed at twelve-thirty by forty-five minutes voting, followed by a late lunch in the self-service canteen and a half an hour to catch up on the papers and the day's news agenda, and to start reading our pre-manifesto document.

Then at three our weekly British Tory delegation meeting commenced, with the pre-manifesto document high on the agenda. At five, I was scheduled to speak in plenary on the proposal for an "industrial observatory" — another day, another quango — but the session was running late and I actually got my two minutes around six o'clock. I had a carefully prepared speech attacking the proposal, to fit my two minutes, but my colleague Giles Chichester who spoke earlier was very keen for me to respond to points made by Labour MEP Stephen Hughes. I got the points in, but it threw my timing and I encountered the President's gavel — not an uncommon occurrence.

I was invited to two cocktail parties between six and eight — British Chambers of Commerce and UNICE, the European employers' organisation — but I didn't have time to do either. Straight on into an Environment Committee meeting at six thirty, and on to a meeting of our EPP/ED Group at seven, where I caused general astonishment by agreeing, for once, with the Christian Democrats, this time on opposing a proposal for tighter restrictions on noise from car tyres. If carried, the proposal would also make tyres dearer, less durable and more dangerous.

During the meeting I got news that the BBC programme Financial World Tonight wanted to interview me. I called them, to find they wanted to do the interview live at 11.30 UK time, half past midnight local time. I was planning to dine with the correspondent of one of our national newspapers, but agreed to come back. We went off to dinner at nine, but I was back in the office by midnight. The BBC call came through around twenty past, and I listened to ten minutes of the programme before speaking on the subject of the Rickety Ladders Directive (no, don't even ask!).

I thought the interview went well, but then I'd had a good dinner, so perhaps I was mistaken. I left the parliament soon after half past midnight. I personally have deep reservations about whether the European Parliament, on balance, does more harm than good. But it's not for want of time or effort.
ﬗﬗﬗ

Of course political life would be nothing without the opposition. This piece from Leap Year's Day 2000

The Slings and Arrows of Political Fortune

In politics, you soon learn to expect attacks from politicians of other parties. Indeed you welcome them, for at least it means that someone has noticed what you're trying to do. Surely the worst possible thing would be to get no reaction at all.

So I suppose I should be grateful for the steady drip-feed of attacks from East Midlands Labour MEP Phillip Whitehead. Actually Phillip is a charming and agreeable chap, a better model for the chuckling uncle than even Frank Dobson – and I daresay he might make a better Mayor of London as well. And it's not all confrontation. In a recent vote in the Environment Committee, Phillip and I joined forces in a show of cross-party solidarity to see off French and Belgian proposals that would have been very damaging for the UK chocolate industry.

Nevertheless, the letters keep coming. Phillip accuses me of playing with the Union Jack in my bath. He's wrong there – although I do have a rather large Union Jack in my Brussels office. He then draws attention to the fact that I wear a Sterling lapel pin, and suggests I might go to a fancy-dress party as a cash register. Since opinion polls show that 69% of the British people want to keep the pound, I should think his letter has done me the world of good. At least they know where I stand. Where does Phillip stand?

He has also calls me a "cod patriot". Now I'm proud to be called a patriot, but I find the reference to cod puzzling. While I have often spoken out for the fishermen, and against the wicked folly of the Common Fisheries Policy, the cod wars were decades ago and I took no part in them.

It's not all negative, though. Phillip was kind enough to call me "straight talking". Can he have got wind of the fact that my last book was called "Straight Talking on Europe", and is he giving me a subtle plug?

But the attacks on the flag and the pound are all of a part with the New Labour project. Tony Blair is setting out to undermine everything that is comfortable and familiar and reassuring. Our counties are subsumed into faceless regions. Our United Kingdom is split into its component parts. The House of Lords is emasculated. The Monarchy is patronised. The Millennium Dome is filled with fatuous nonsense and lacks any reference to our history, our culture or our achievements.

The plan is clear – to deny us our identity and heritage, and turn us loose rootless and rudderless in Labour's Brave New Euro-World.

Liberal MEP Nick Clegg takes a different tack. He fulminates against those who "want to turn their backs on Europe". I have a challenge for him. Who are these people who want to turn their backs on Europe? I honestly cannot think of anyone who takes that view. The dishonest campaign by Britain in Europe claiming that "3 million jobs are at risk" seems to suggest that the choice is either to join the Euro or stop trading with Europe. That's a totally daft and false choice. Every politician that I know of agrees that we want to co-operate and trade with our European partners. That's not the question. The question is, do we want to be governed by our own democratically-elected representatives in Westminster, or by unaccountable bureaucrats in Brussels?

America, Japan, China all trade with the EU without joining the Euro. Why do Nick Clegg and Britain in Europe think that we need to join the sinking Euro to trade with Europe? ❧❧❧

As of the end of 2001, I had made two substantial trips outside the EU on parliamentary business, one to Asia, my old stomping ground, as a member of the ASEAN + Korea parliamentary delegation, and the other to the USA on a delegation from the Temporary Committee on Bioethics and Human Genetics. Both were fascinating experiences.

Asia Visit, May 2000

I have just returned from a European Parliament visit to Asia – Singapore & Malaysia. I write this with uncharacteristic trepidation, because I'm not sure that taxpayers will feel that the cost was worthwhile. Five MEPs – and the inevitable five staff members – made the trip at about £5,000 each (the airfare was over £3,000), so the total cost will be around £50,000. I thought hard about whether I should go, but as it was going ahead anyhow, it seemed better to have one Euro-realist on the visit rather than none.

The objective of visits like this, which take place all over the world, is to build relationships between parliamentarians of the EU and other countries. I was particularly interested to go to South East Asia, as I spent around twelve years of my business career out there.

We met the Prime Minister of Singapore, and other government ministers and MPs from both countries. We attended a session of the Singapore Parliament, designed very much on the Westminster model. One parliamentary question dealt with was something called "killer litter laws". Now, I know that they hang drug dealers in Singapore, but litter louts?! It turned out to be a reference to a couple of cases where residents had thrown out old TVs from high-rise buildings, with unfortunate results.

We also visited the Monetary Authority of Singapore (MAS) which is effectively their Central Bank. I had the opportunity to ask a question which was designed (I admit it!) to wrong-foot my federast colleagues.

I recalled the fact that Singapore has been united with Malaysia in 1963 but separated into independent states in 1965. From 1963 to 1965 they shared a common currency – the Malaysian dollar. After 1965, they split this into two currencies – the Malaysian dollar & the Singapore dollar (the Sing dollar is now worth about double the Malay dollar). Could they explain to me, I asked, how they handled the difficult technical task of separating out the two currencies when citizens of both states had identical notes and coins in their pockets? The experience of MAS, I added, might be helpful for members of the Eurozone if and when they are forced to break up the Euro into national currencies!

You could almost hear the sharp intake of breath. Four MEPs and five staffers could see where the question was going, but could do nothing to stop it. The answer was interesting. Malaysia & Singapore agreed to hold the two currencies at parity for seven years, while they changed the old coins & notes for new ones. After that, they floated against one another.

Amazingly, Commission President Prodi has recently said that if Britain should join the Euro, it would not be impossible to withdraw later. But pressure for withdrawal would arise because exchange rates and interest rates were clearly unsustainable, and we would not have the luxury of a seven-year change-over period. Prodi is right – it would be possible to leave the Euro. But it would be hugely expensive and disruptive. Much better not to join in the first place.

One minister in Malaysia remarked on the benefits that the country has enjoyed from its colonial legacy. Democracy, education, accountancy and the legal system are all very much based on the British model. I noticed also that the Asians we met were mostly much clearer and more fluent in English than most of my continental colleagues. Indeed, I find Singapore & Kuala Lumpur (KL) a good deal less foreign than Brussels and Strasbourg.

In KL, we met EBIC, the European Business Information Centre, a sort of EU Chamber of Commerce. The various EU businessmen we met were deeply angry. The EU Commission had apparently agreed funding for EBIC but despite repeated appeals has failed to deliver any money. It was lost in the system. Meantime, the Secretary of EBIC had had to borrow from the bank on his own security, and was personally liable for something like £20,000. We agreed to follow this up with the Commission, but we were fairly horrified. This is how banana republics operate, not what claims to be the greatest economic bloc in the world.

We were horrified, but not surprised. I constantly hear stories of individuals and companies owed money by the Commission and unpaid for several months or years. And Commissioner Chris Patten has just gone on record as saying that it will take many years to deliver the existing aid promises that the Commission has littered around the world like confetti.

At the Asia-Europe Institute in Singapore, I heard a German bureaucrat praising the EU model of integration as an example for ASEAN (the Association of South East Asian Nations) to follow. His arrogance and complacency were practically neo-colonialist. I squirmed with embarrassment for his Asian colleagues. I replied:

"Here we are in Singapore, which has a per capita GDP higher than any EU country except Luxembourg. Everything is clean, everything works. There is (notwithstanding killer-litter!) very little crime, no unemployment, no underclass. Singapore is a shining example of a successful 21st Century City. I believe that we have more to learn from them than vice versa."

Afterwards, over lunch, one of the Asian colleagues quietly thanked me for putting the record straight.

Our final visit was to Malaysia's Multi-Media Super Highway, a fully wired-up complex stretching from KL to the new airport, including the new government administrative centre of Putrajaya as well as the IT industrial complex, Cyberjaya. This is designed to jump-start Malaysia into the internet age and it looks set to be a big success. They are attracting major global investors, developing physical and electronic infrastructure and putting great emphasis on IT education at all levels.

Several key points were raised during the presentation. They recognise that the internet means a borderless world where companies can do business across town or the across the globe, a world where the global language is English and where geography is less and less relevant. What a lesson here for the EU. Being close to the European continent is just an accident of geography, and is increasingly irrelevant in economic terms. Rather than locking ourselves ever closer into the most inward-looking, over-regulated and over-taxed bloc in the world, we should look to wider horizons and focus on our traditional role as a global trading nation.

In the same presentation they showed a graph illustrating the dramatic reduction in transaction costs as a result of e-commerce. That single graph exploded one of the few half-genuine arguments for the UK joining the Euro – that it will reduce transaction costs. But that's happening anyway. We have much to learn from Asia, not least their outward-looking focus on growth, trade and productivity. Perhaps my visit was worth it after all. ༄༅༄

USA Visit: Pro-life or Pro-choice?

The European Parliament broke up for the summer on July 12th (2001) and the next week several groups of MEPs were on their way to Washington. Indeed there were so many, we almost had a quorum. I was flying across the Atlantic as part of the parliament's Committee on Human Genetics – at about the same time as President Bush was flying the other way to have lunch with the Queen.

Our mission: to check out the state of the scientific, ethical and political debate in the USA on human genetics. And our timing was perfect. It was the hot issue of the week. Every time we switched on CNN or opened a copy of USA Today, the top story was "stem cell research". Would President Bush authorise federal funding for research on human embryos, or not?

Just in case you're thinking this all sounds a bit like a gravy-train jolly, let me remark in passing that we worked fifteen-hour days, starting at 7:30 a.m. and including working lunches and dinners. We were definitely in breach of the Working Time Directive!

We were briefed by the EU Commission delegation and by the British Embassy. We met experts at the National Bioethics Advisory Council, and visited Celera Genomics. This company was a key player in the Human Genome Project. We saw dozens of Jurassic-Park-style gene sequencing machines, which hum away 24 hours a day, sequencing DNA for everything from bacteria to fruit flies to human beings.

Then lunch with the National Institute for Health, before we set off to Capitol Hill to meet with senators and congressmen (passing Hilary Clinton in the corridor!). The first full day ended with a dinner with the American Association for the Advancement of Science, where we debated the issues over dinner before each of three tables briefed the meeting on our conclusions – I spoke for table #3.

Thursday saw us at the Cold Spring Harbour Laboratory on Long Island Sound. Many of the buildings on their campus are picture-postcard colonial houses, on lawns below the tree-line that sweep down to the marina in this former whaling harbour. There we met Dr. James Watson, grand old man of modern genetics. With Francis Crick, he discovered the spiral structure of DNA, at Cambridge in 1953. Chatting to him over lunch, we found that he had left Cambridge in 1962 – the same year that I went there to study for my maths degree.

Then we went on to Boston, for meetings with Harvard University and MIT, the Massachusetts Institute of Technology.

We were looking at a range of issues – using genetics to reduce the risk of mothers having disabled children; whether genetic research should be patented; whether genetic tests should affect employment or insurance opportunities – but the biggest issue was embryonic stem cell research.

Millions of couples around the world have been given hope and joy as a result of IVF fertility treatment. But this inevitably creates more embryos than are eventually used. So the vexed moral question comes down to this. What do we do with these spare embryos? Do we flush them down the loo? Or do we use them for research that may provide cures for Parkinson's, for cancer or heart disease? Put like that, the question answers itself.

One of my MEP colleagues has Parkinson's. For him, it's literally a matter of life and death. Do we deny him the hope of a cure because of moral scruples about embryos that will be destroyed anyway?

One convinced anti-abortion, anti-research Senator, Sam Brownback, insisted on describing microscopic 48-hour embryos as "young human beings". I asked him if he regarded his breakfast egg as "a young chicken". The debate in the US has rather polarised around the abortion issue – pro-life versus pro-choice. But interestingly, several key pro-lifers, including Senator Orrin Hatch, whose staff we met, have supported research despite their anti-abortion position.

This debate matters not only for health, but for business too. At least one California research company is planning to come to the UK if US regulation gets too oppressive in this area.

So where do I stand? Well I guess I'm pro-life. But I'm pro-quality, not pro-quantity. So that makes me pro-choice too. ❧❧❧

Quote from William Hague's Conference Speech

Just because Tony Blair is paranoid about the forces of conservatism, that doesn't mean we're not out to get him

Chapter seventeen

Plenary Speeches

Plenary sessions of the parliament take place each month in Strasbourg, although the parliament now has such an enormous volume of business that extra "mini-plenaries" are scheduled for Brussels as well. This is where much of the voting takes place, and we may vote a thousand times in a week. That may represent only twenty or so reports, but each may have hundreds of amendments. The votes take place at breakneck speed, and although generally we know what a few key votes are about (and final votes on important reports), it is impossible to be familiar with all the amendments — so we rely on the spokesmen and the whips to advise us.

The plenary debates are almost as sterile and formulaic as the votes. Most speakers are allowed a mere two minutes — sometimes less — and the time limit is fairly strictly enforced. There is no real debate or too-and-fro, and MEPs for the most part are simply reading their speech into the record as a peg for a later press release. Indeed the debates are very poorly attended, which enabled us to mount the ambush described in Chapter 4 ("European political parties").

However, because of the time limit, the plenary speech becomes something of a challenge. No room for waffle or generalisation. In my experience, around 250 words is the maximum safe limit — and I don't speak slowly! Every word must count, and, as I like to think of it, every sentence must contain a hand-grenade. Here are some examples.

The Buitenveg report, in May 2000, was about equal opportunities in employment. To achieve this objective, it proposed a major change to a fundamental legal principle. It moved the burden of proof from the accuser to the accused.

Speech, Buitenveg Report, May 18th 2000

In mediæval times, groups of thugs and hooligans would pick on elderly women and accuse them of witchcraft. They would throw them into the village pond. If the poor souls drowned, that showed they were innocent. If they survived, it proved their guilt, and they were burned at the stake. Either way, they ended up dead.

In twentieth century China, during the cultural revolution, Red Guards would accuse intellectuals of bourgeois thinking. If they confessed, they were guilty but redeemable. But if they denied the charge, they were condemned out of their own mouths, because they had failed to recognise their guilt.

In both these cases we see the danger of placing the burden of proof on the accused. Our justice systems have always rightly placed the burden of proof on the accuser, not on the defendant, they have always assumed that a person is innocent until proven guilty.

Now, in twenty-first century Europe, we propose to abandon this fundamental principle of justice, and instead to adopt the approach of the mediæval witch-finders or the Chinese Red Guards. We propose to put the burden of proof on the defendant, and we even have amendments that would further pass the benefit of the doubt to the accuser, not the accused.

Before entering politics, I worked for a third of a century in industry, and I have hired hundreds of people. I worked for many years in Asia, and I have hired many Chinese, Malays, Thais and Koreans. In the textile business which I ran in Leicester until last year, there was a high proportion of employees from South Asia. I am very positive about hiring members of ethnic minorities.

But I also know that when an employer has a short list of similarly-qualified candidates, it is often impossible to provide an objective justification for selecting one candidate rather than another. It will thus be impossible for the employer to defend himself if an unsuccessful candidate from an ethnic minority makes a claim of discrimination.

Even if the employer mounts a successful defence, the time and the anxiety of a tribunal or court hearing will be a huge imposition. And given the bias of this legislation in favour of the accuser, and the prevailing climate of political correctness, even innocent employers will frequently lose their cases, incurring penalties as well as court costs and lost time. This legislation is an invitation to troublemakers and those with chips on their shoulders to bring frivolous and vexatious complaints, or possibly to use the threat of a complaint to secure financial compensation.

There is another danger, and that is that employers, aware of the risks of complaints from unsuccessful ethnic minority candidates, may avoid putting them on short lists. As so often with legislation in this house, we have failed to think through the possible unintended consequences.

This legislation is unnecessary at the European level – member states have their own anti-discrimination measures designed to suit their own culture and circumstances. This proposed transfer of the burden of proof to the accused is a gross affront to natural justice. It will be a huge new burden on businesses, including the SMEs that we pretend to support. It will be a field day for the witch-hunters and zealots of the race relations industry. I appeal to all right-minded colleagues to reject it. ❧❧❧

The Arvidsson report dealt with an unpronounceable chemical substance — phthalate — which is an important plasticiser for polythene.

Arvidsson Report – Phthalates — 5th September, 2000

Mr. President: So much has gone wrong on the phthalates issue that it is difficult to know where to start. The Commission's temporary bans have no legal basis. The Commission may introduce an emergency ban where there is a clear and immediate danger, but no such danger exists with phthalates.

These materials have been in widespread, general use around the world for forty years, and yet there is no evidence of any kind that any damage has ever been done to anyone. There was one test on rats in which massive quantities of phthalates appeared to cause problems, but no one has been able to replicate the test. We are dealing here with little more than media hysteria and ignorance.

Compare and contrast our position on phthalates with our position on tobacco. Phthalates have done no harm to anyone, ever, yet we are banning them. Tobacco, we are told, kills half a million people each year in the EU. Do we ban it? NO! We subsidise it with a billion Euros.

If we ban phthalates, alternative materials of which we have less experience may prove to be a greater risk. This has already happened, for example, with breast implants, where alternatives to silicon have proved more dangerous than the implants they replaced.

In trying to defend an untenable position, the Commission has shamelessly sought to gag its own scientific advisers. It has bowdlerised their reports, and pressured them into changing their positions. Honesty and transparency have been sacrificed to expedience. I and other colleagues wrote to Commission President Prodi on this point two months ago. I understand that his reply has been held for some time "awaiting signature" – presumably to ensure that we should not see it before today's votes.

Neither the temporary bans nor the permanent ban are justified by the evidence. Migration tests for phthalates are currently under development and will probably be available within months. We should wait until these tests are available, and then, if we must, impose migration limits.

We hear far too much about the "precautionary principle". To be meaningful, the precautionary principle should be invoked only when there is a clear and demonstrable risk. If we continue to invoke it when there is no *prima facie* risk at all, we make both the precautionary principle, and ourselves, look ridiculous. ༺༝༺༝

When the EU can, it will create a regulation. If not, it will often propose an "observatory" — a new bureaucracy which will produce reports in eleven languages — reports that as likely as not will gather dust on a shelf. But never mind. The MEPs can go home with a warm feeling that they've **done something** *about a perceived problem. In September 2000 there was a proposal for an "Industrial Observatory" which would monitor labour standards and issues across the EU.*

The Industrial Observatory, September 5th 2000

Mr. President: Before I start on the subject of the Observatory, may I make a general point to the Commission. They are bringing forward far too much legislation, and with legislation, quality is usually in inverse proportion to quantity. We talk of doing less and doing it better. In fact, we are doing more and doing it worse.

I was deeply disheartened to hear of the proposal for this observatory. The rule seems to be, another day, another quango. For the benefit of colleagues I should perhaps explain that "Quango" is a recently coined English word. It is short for Quasi Non-Governmental Organisation. In other words, a new piece of bureaucracy, more money spent, more jobs for the boys, more patronage for their bosses. And all for what? To produce fat reports which will be translated into eleven languages, but which nobody will read.

We seem to have only two responses in the EU to any real or imagined problem. We either create a new regulation, without any concern as to whether existing regulations are working uniformly, fairly or effectively. Or we create an observatory. Then we stand back, proud and happy that we have solved the problem. Generally, we haven't solved it at all. We've simply postponed it. We've wasted time and money. And we've raised expectations which will never be fulfilled. No wonder the public are fast becoming disillusioned with the European project.

As with so many EU initiatives (I think particularly of the proposed Food Standards Agency), this Observatory will simply duplicate the work of other organisations — of innumerable private research companies and accountancy firms, of academic and university institutes, of trade unions and chambers of commerce, and of national and local government.

I put two questions to colleagues. First, do we really need this observatory at all? I think not. But if we do, would it not be far quicker, cheaper and more cost-effective to commission one of our great European accounting firms to do the work? I am sure it would. ❧❧❧

When I first came to the parliament, I thought I would spend my time doing battle with the Commission. But although the Commission does much that I deprecate, it will usually check its plans with industry, and at least make some kind of sense, before it promulgates a legislative proposal. All too often, the parliament will then table ludicrous amendments, and I find that I am voting against the parliamentary amendments, and thus (by default) in favour of the Commission position. Better the frying pan than the fire!

Why not table amendments that make the Commission position better, you may well ask? Well we can, and sometimes we do, if we see any chance of winning. But in the prevailing socialist, federalist climate of the institutions, amendments which favour industry or incline towards common sense have little chance of surviving.

Here is a good example:

Car Tyre Noise, September 9th 2000

Mr. President: Before I start on the subject of tyre noise, may I make a general point to the Commission. They are bringing forward far too much legislation, and with legislation, quality is usually in inverse proportion to quantity. We talk of doing less and doing it better. In fact, we are doing more and doing it worse.

Now turning to tyres: I little thought when I came to this house that I should end up defending the Commission's position. And yet the Commission has done its homework. It has consulted with the industry. It has come up with a proposal that sets challenging but achievable targets, which protects the environment while also recognising the interests of road users and tyre makers.

Now some of our colleagues seek to sabotage this careful work by demanding arbitrary and ill-considered decibel reductions. In some cases their figures are achievable, in other not. But they have forgotten that changes in the production specifications of tyres affect not only noise, but also grip, safety, cost and durability. They may end up with quieter tyres that are expensive, that wear out quickly, and that allow cars to slide off the road and crash into trees. Let me speak plainly: more road users will die if these amendments are passed. The electors that I represent will not thank us.

We are being far too prescriptive. It is our job to set a broad legislative framework in the public interest. Instead we seek to micro-manage a highly technical and complex industrial development programme — a task for which we have neither the time nor the skills.

I call on colleagues to reject the amendments and support the Commission's proposal. ❧❧❧

The debate on the Lisbon summit took place in April 2000, and I was outraged by a speech that the President of the parliament, Nicole Fontaine, had made at the summit. She is a member of the EPP group to which we Tories are allied — but we have strange bedfellows.

Lisbon Summit

Madame President:

Many commentators have drawn comparisons between the European Union and the Soviet Union. Both have been profoundly anti-democratic. Both have seemed opposed to enterprise and wealth creation. At the Lisbon summit it appeared that the EU had rediscovered a commitment to enterprise. Although I have some reservations about references to the social market in this resolution, I am happy to support it. Let us hope that it is carried through into effect, and is more than mere sound-bites and press releases.

However you yourself, Madame President, made a remarkable speech in Lisbon which amounted to a virulent and vituperative attack on multinational companies, on liberal economics, on free markets, on the very heart of Western capitalism.

I have no doubt that you were prompted by the best of humanitarian intentions, but you must understand that if your proposals were carried out, they would damage competitiveness and productivity, they would deter investment, they would hurt prosperity, and above all they would increase unemployment in Europe. You are attacking nothing less than the foundations of Western capitalism, the engine which has delivered wealth and success undreamed of by earlier generations.

You said that European people are "scandalised by untrammelled capitalism, whose relocations, social dumping, ruthless exploitation, and remorseless pursuit of profit at the expense of working men and women have a direct and traumatic effect on their lives".

This goes beyond socialism. It is pure Marxism. It may have been appropriate for the Kremlin in the 60s, but it is totally out of place in 21st century Europe.

It is typical of this parliament that we call for an end to unemployment, yet we take actions that have the opposite effect. Your remarks fit this depressing tradition perfectly.

I don't know whether you were speaking for your party, for the parliament, or in a personal capacity. But I absolutely reject, repudiate and condemn your comments, and I am delighted to have this opportunity of publicly dissociating myself from them. ✍✍✍

The Karas report proposed spending tax-payers' money on what amounts to a propaganda campaign for the euro. I thought that this was a bad idea.

Speech on KARAS – Euro Propaganda — July 4th, 2000

Mr. President

As I and many colleagues have argued for some time, the EMU project is profoundly dangerous. It is economically naïve, and will do huge macro-economic damage. Politically, it is clearly intended to undermine the nation state and thus it threatens democracy in Europe.

The proposal before us talks of information on the Euro. But we already have all the information we need. Every newspaper I open has stories on the Euro. Banks and accountancy firms are running seminars and briefing clients. This is not about information. It is about propaganda. I do not trust the Commission to provide unbiased information – the very idea is absurd.

Now if the twelve Euro countries wish to undertake a propaganda campaign, that is no business of mine. But in three countries, Denmark, Sweden and Great Britain, the Euro decision is not yet made. It would be a gross abuse of the democratic process for the Commission to undertake a Euro propaganda campaign in those countries before referenda on the currency take place. It would be outrageous to take money from the taxpayer and to use it to influence the voters' decision.

In Britain, 70% of people are opposed to joining the Euro. We do not want our money spent promoting it, either in the UK or elsewhere. I therefore have two demands to make of the Commission.

First, please tell us today that no such campaign will be undertaken in Great Britain, Denmark or Sweden. Secondly, please assure us that the share of funding which might have been spent in those countries is returned to their national exchequers, so that the people can see, clearly and transparently, that their money has not be squandered on objectives they do not support.

Better still, cancel the whole project, and put all the funds into a special account to help defray the enormous costs that will be incurred when the Euro is eventually dismantled. ✍✍✍

Chapter eighteen

Where is the EU Going?

After seventeen chapters dealing (mostly!) with where Europe is now, and with more-or-less current developments, it might be interesting to conclude with a look a little further ahead. What will the EU look like for our children and grandchildren? Must we resign ourselves to our new provincial status on the remote north-western fringes of the nation of Europe — or can we cheer on those who (to quote the strap-line of the euro-sceptic magazine "These Tides") are "Working for the post-EU Europe"?

This first piece reviews an alarming paper on the long-term demographics of Europe.

The Spectre Haunting Europe

A spectre of catastrophe is looming over continental Europe. It will be twenty to thirty years before its effects are felt substantially, but it is inexorable and probably unavoidable. It is the threat of a massive decline in population, coupled with an even more dramatic and damaging reduction in the work-force. With a plunging birth-rate and increasing longevity, each worker will be supporting relatively more pensioners, within a shrinking economy. Pension and health-care costs will spiral out of control.

UN population estimates suggest that the population of Germany may decline from 82 million (1995) to 56 million (2050), a drop of over 30%, while the percentage of pensioners will rise from 16% to 30%. The figures for Italy show a drop of a third, from 57 to 38 million, with a rise in the proportion of pensioners from 17 to 34%.

How can anyone know what will happen in 2050? Changes in population take place over very long periods, and today's birth-rate tells us a lot about future population. For example, of Britain's future work-force in 2050, a third are already born. Even a sudden up-surge in birth-rate (of which there is no sign) would take decades to work through the system.

Why is population declining? There are lots of reasons. In the opulent west, educated young women are pursuing careers, couples are marrying later, having fewer children and having them later. In Eastern Europe, the opposite applies – poverty and economic despair, coupled with readily available abortion, have driven the birth-rate down.

For a generation raised on the threat of global over-population, the idea of a decline may seem a novelty – even a welcome relief. The so-called "pensions time-bomb", as the ratio of retired people to workers increases, has had some coverage in the media, but is only a fraction of the problem.

A smaller population will buy fewer cars, fewer 'fridges, fewer goods and services generally. The economy will shrink as both the work-force and population shrink. This is why global financial markets, and even major European companies, are investing in America, in Asia, indeed everywhere except in Europe. This is one reason for the euro's collapse.

One country bucks the trend: Turkey. Its population is set to rise from 62 million (1995) to 106 million (2050), a huge increase of 70%, while its percent of pensioners in 2050 will only be around 15%. There is currently a debate about whether Turkey should be admitted to the EU. If it is, then it will be the EU's largest country by 2050, with a work-force greater than Germany and France combined. The EU's centre of gravity will move inexorably eastwards.

If the EU has any underlying cultural values at all, surely its foundation is the Judeo-Christian tradition. Many people might be concerned to find that an Islamic country had become the dominant member-state of the EU.

EU leaders are aware of a population disaster in the making. One suggested solution is massive immigration. But immigration on the scale required could put great strains on existing social structures. And we have to question the morality of inviting the brightest and best in developing countries to leave home for Europe.

Fortunately, this thunder-cloud has a silver lining, at least for the UK. We are not immune to these trends, but they started earlier for us and will develop more slowly. They are manageable. Our population is set to drop only 17% by 2050, and the percent of pensioners to rise from 16% to 22%. The fact that most of our pension plans are fully-funded will be a huge help.

Britain, in fact, is a life-boat alongside a sinking Europe. But to ensure that our life-boat stays afloat, it is vital that we put a halt to economic integration with the continent, and above all that we keep control of our own currency, monetary policy and taxation. In other words, it is vital that we should not join the euro. If we did, we should simply be buying-in to Europe's coming melt-down.

Britain is a global trading nation. We should not allow ourselves to become an off-shore province in a Europe facing demographic disaster. ❧❧❧

See "The Death of Europe", by Anthony Scholefield, Futurus, 0208 782
1135

This last article, from February 2001, brings together two ideas — the Conservative objective of global free trade by 2020, and the fact that the EU, if it survives, will be seventy years old by then. Perhaps appropriately, the piece starts with the same trompe l'oeil *idea that opened the first piece in the book, my speech to the Democracy Movement in Matlock — the parallel between the EU and the USSR. That was from about the same time (January 2001), so clearly I thought the paragraph from the speech good enough to recycle in a press article. But this time I took the parallel one step further.*

Will the EU Exist in 2020?

They thought they could submerge proud and ancient nations into a new power bloc. They thought they could ride roughshod over the instincts and aspirations of ordinary people. They thought they could impose uniform employment and social policies across a continent. They thought they could create a mighty state that would challenge the global hegemony of the USA.

I am writing, of course, about the Soviet Union, but you could be forgiven for noticing the parallels with the European Union. No metaphor should be pushed too far, and if we study the details there are wide differences between the USSR and the EU. And yet the similarities are too close for comfort.

I have often pointed out that the EU's Common Agricultural Policy is the last example of Soviet-style central planning still in captivity. It is beyond reform and deserves to be put out of its misery.

But new developments in the EU's on-going drive for integration – the Treaty of Nice and the so-called Charter of Fundamental Rights – contain profoundly troubling echoes of Communist and Nazi totalitarian régimes.

The Treaty of Nice provides for pan-European political parties with tax-payers' funding. Worse still, it envisages powers for the EU to act against political parties that are not sufficiently committed to the EU's ideals. These proposals are clearly aimed at the right-wing Austrian Freedom Party. But who is to say that they would not be used against British Euro-sceptic parties, like UKIP or even a Euro-sceptic Tory party?

Indeed the EU's funding proposals already discriminate against the Conservatives. Labour is part of the European Socialist Party, and would therefore qualify for EU funding (paid for out of your taxes). But the Conservatives are not part of any trans-national party, and so would not qualify for funding. And don't forget that the Labour government's one-sided proposals for a Euro referendum would also allow EU funding for the YES campaign.

The right of the EU to take action against political parties is reminiscent of Eastern Europe in the bad old days. They never banned elections. They just banned parties that disagreed with the state.

But the so-called Charter of Fundamental Rights is even more dangerous. Of course our rights as Englishmen and women derive not from politicians or governments or Charters, but from the long evolution of our democracy and common law. But now along comes Europe and says, in effect, "Oh no, you are not born with your rights. You are given them by the EU. And not even given. They are only lent, and we can take them back when we see fit".

Article 52 of the Charter states that the EU can suspend your rights whenever it wants. No due process, no challenges allowed. This is the so-called *raison d'état,* or reason of state, beloved of East German constitutional lawyers, which allows your rights to be suspended. As my colleague Dan Hannan MEP has written, the ability of a state to suspend its own constitution is the defining characteristic of a tyranny. Hitler's Nazi constitution for Germany had just such a clause.

The EU is not just a threat to our prosperity. It is a direct challenge to our freedom and democracy. The roots of democracy in Europe are fragile. Most of the major EU member states have had totalitarian régimes in my lifetime.

The only benefit of the EU is free trade between the member states. I wish I had a pound for everyone in the East Midlands who has said to me "We voted in 1975 for a Common Market, for free trade. Not for this political monster". The Conservative Party has called for global free trade by 2020. If global free trade is achieved, then the EU will have outlived its usefulness and, like the state in Marxist theory, should simply wither away.

Coincidentally, the 2020 date has another significance, if we follow through the USSR/EU metaphor. The USSR lasted for around 70 years, before it collapsed under the weight of its internal inconsistencies. The EU, in one form or another, has been around for fifty years. If it follows the same pattern, 2020 could be the year when the EU finally fades away, and freedom and democracy will be secure.

Clement Attlee was the post-war Labour Prime Minister (1945/51). In the last year of his life, 1967, tiny and frail, he was helped onto the platform to address an anti-Common Market group of Labour MPs. Noted for his brevity, he spoke as follows: "The Common Market. The so-called Common Market of six nations. Know them well. Very recently this country spent a great deal of blood and treasure rescuing four of 'em from attacks by the other two".